MANIFEST

7 STEPS TO LIVING
YOUR BEST LIFE

ROXIE NAFOUSI

MICHAEL  JOSEPH

MICHAEL JOSEPH

UK | USA | Canada | Ireland | Australia
India | New Zealand | South Africa

Michael Joseph is part of the Penguin Random House group of companies
whose addresses can be found at global.penguinrandomhouse.com

Penguin
Random House
UK

First published 2022
001

Copyright © Roxie Nafousi, 2022

The moral right of the author has been asserted

Cover design based on a concept by Amy Bailey

Every effort has been made to trace copyright holders and to obtain their
permission where required for the use of copyright material. The publisher
apologizes for any errors or omissions and would be grateful to be notified of
any corrections that should be incorporated in future editions of this book

Set in 10/12.5pt Garamond MT Pro
Typeset by Jouve (UK), Milton Keynes
Printed and bound in Great Britain by Clays Ltd, Elcograf S.p.A.

The authorized representative in the EEA is Penguin Random House Ireland,
Morrison Chambers, 32 Nassau Street, Dublin D02 YH68

A CIP catalogue record for this book is available from the British Library

ISBN: 978–0–241–53959–0

www.greenpenguin.co.uk

MIX
Paper from
responsible sources
FSC   FSC® C018179
www.fsc.org

Penguin Random House is committed to a
sustainable future for our business, our readers
and our planet. This book is made from Forest
Stewardship Council® certified paper.

For my son, Wolfe
Be whoever you want to be

CONTENTS

INTRODUCTION

TO MANIFEST:
To make something happen

Manifesting is the ability to create the exact life that you want. It is the ability to draw in anything that you desire and become the author of your own story. It looks and feels like magic, and we are all the magicians.

MY MANIFESTING JOURNEY

In May 2018, my life looked entirely different to how it does now. I was twenty-seven years old and I had no idea what I wanted to do with my life; I had no job, no direction and no sense of purpose. I had been in a battle with depression for over a decade, and in the grip of addiction for almost as long. I was overwhelmingly sad for much of the time, my self-worth was non-existent and, after a string of failed relationships, I was very much alone.

I had just returned from Thailand, where I had gone for a month to complete a yoga teacher-training course. I had gone in hope that not only would I get a qualification I could potentially use to assemble some sort of career but also that, in being away from the temptations of city life, I would be able to heal my pain and change my hedonistic, partying ways. But I was back in London for less than twenty-four hours before I found myself in the same old cycle; smoking, drinking and taking drugs. It was then – and not for the first time – that I hit rock bottom. I felt completely hopeless. If not even a month of

1

self-reflection, daily meditation, clean eating and two hundred hours of yoga could help me, what would?

I called my friend Sophia, totally broken. When would I ever feel happy? I asked her. She said to me, 'I listened to a podcast on something called manifesting last night. I'll send you the link now, I think it could really help you.' I was on my way to get a manicure at the time, so I figured that while I sat and had my nails reapplied I may as well just put on my headphones and listen. As I recollect this story now, I have such a vivid image in my mind; I can see myself sitting in the white chair, wearing my black leggings and oversized denim jacket, having my nails painted a candy-coloured pink as I listened intently to something that was about to change my world for ever.

When my nails were done I went straight home and opened up my laptop. I typed into Google, 'What is manifesting?' and I sat and read and researched and listened and learned and absorbed everything I could on manifesting. I already knew the first thing I wanted to manifest: unconditional love.

Just one week after listening to that podcast episode and putting into practice some of the things I had learned, I received a message on a dating app called Raya from an Australian actor named Wade Briggs. We had no friends in common, but I thought he looked particularly cute and so I replied, and we quickly began a non-stop texting marathon.

Two weeks later, Wade happened to be stopping in London for four days after travelling through Europe in a van for several months with his best friend, before heading back home to Australia. So we decided to meet up the day after he arrived in the city.

Our date went so well that Wade decided not to get on his flight home so that he could just 'stay a bit longer and see what happens'.

Three months later, we found out I was pregnant.

On 7 June 2019, exactly one year *to the day* after receiving his message, our baby boy, Wolfe, was born. **There it was: unconditional love.**

Three years later, Wade and I are stronger than ever, and totally and utterly obsessed with our perfect little boy. On top of that, I am free of all addiction, I have carved out a successful career for myself which is full of purpose and passion, I am happier and more content than I could put into words and I finally possess something I thought would be forever out of my reach: self-love.

After discovering manifesting, I took everything I learned and, almost instinctively, organized it in my mind into seven simple steps. I started following the steps myself and then everything began to unfold in the most magnificent and rapid way. The change felt so magical, yet at the same time it made so much sense to me that it felt entirely logical, too. My life transformed in every way imaginable; not an inch of it was left the same. And it all happened because of one thing: understanding the true art of manifestation.

I started telling all my friends, and my small following on Instagram, about this incredible thing called 'manifesting'. Most people had no idea what I was talking about and those that did always said the same thing: 'Oh, isn't that when you just visualize what you want and it happens?' I realized then that the majority of people had never even heard about manifesting, and those that had only seemed to understand the surface layer of it: that was why so few people were successfully doing it.

I felt this urge, a calling within me, to teach as many people as possible how to uncover the power that lies within them. Over the last two years I have shared my 7-step guide to manifesting with thousands and thousands of men and women in my workshops and webinars. I receive daily messages from people who have transformed their worlds and made their dreams come true, thanks to this powerful and magical practice. As we entered 2021, I knew that it was time to write this book, because I knew that I could reach – and teach – so many more people through the written word.

I continue to use manifestation every single day, and I live and breathe the steps I am going to teach you. It serves me in all the best ways and enables me to wake up every single day both grateful for all that I have and excited about what the universe is going to bring to me.

Since starting my workshops, I have seen a rise in interest in manifesting, and this interest has certainly been gaining momentum. It has been so exciting to see more and more people opening their minds to the idea that they are in charge of their destiny, but, for many people, the amount of information can be overwhelming and it can be hard to know where to begin. Within this book, I have streamlined *everything you need to know* into 7 simple steps so that you can unlock the magic for yourself and begin your journey to manifesting your dream life.

I want to say this, though, loud and clear: manifesting is so much more than just a trend. **Manifesting is a meeting of science and wisdom; it is a philosophy to live by and a self-development practice to help you live your best life.**

Manifesting is not a new concept. William Walker Atkinson introduced the concept of manifestation in his book *Thought Vibration or the Law of Attraction in the Thought World,* all the way back in 1906. And one of my favourite definitions of manifesting was written in 1937, by journalist Napoleon Hill, in *Think and Grow Rich*. He said 'You are the master of your destiny. You can influence, direct and control your own environment. You can make your life what you want it to be.' Since then, many great philosophers and thinkers have gone on to write about the power of manifesting: some of my favourite teachers include Louise Hay, Abraham Hicks, Wayne Dyer, Eckhart Tolle, Oprah Winfrey and Dr Joe Dispenza.

All these people know something that I now know, too, without any doubt: *manifesting works.*

THE SCIENCE OF MANIFESTING

I said just now that manifesting was the meeting of science and wisdom. So here is a simplified explanation of the science for you.

Quantum physics has taught us that everything in the universe is made up of energy. We are made up of energy, the chair we sit on is energy and the sky above us is all energy too. In other words, all physical matter is pure energy. What differentiates one thing from another is the vibrational frequency and the density of the atoms it is constituted from. The frequency of the vibration can be high, low or anywhere in between.

The law of attraction states that **like attracts like**. This means that a high-frequency vibration attracts high-frequency vibrations back to it, and a low-frequency vibration attracts low-frequency vibrations back to it.

Our thoughts, emotions and feelings are all made up of energy, too, and different emotions have different frequencies. When we change our thoughts, we change how we feel and what emotions we experience, which in turn shifts our entire vibrational frequency. We then attract back to us the frequency that we put

5

out. So, if we alter our thoughts, and therefore our emotions, we can alter our vibration and, ultimately, our reality.

Throughout this book, I will use the terms 'high vibe' and 'low vibe' to describe the high or low frequency of the vibration.

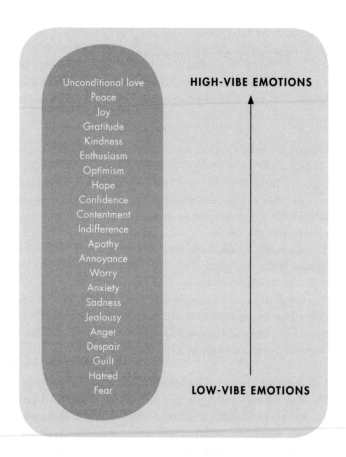

HIGH-VIBE EMOTIONS

Unconditional love
Peace
Joy
Gratitude
Kindness
Enthusiasm
Optimism
Hope
Confidence
Contentment
Indifference
Apathy
Annoyance
Worry
Anxiety
Sadness
Jealousy
Anger
Despair
Guilt
Hatred
Fear

LOW-VIBE EMOTIONS

The science of manifesting works in another way, too, that is less about quantum physics and much more about neuroscience. The idea is that we can use neuroplasticity (our brain's ability to change and form new pathways through growth, learning and experience) to raise our subconscious feelings of self-worth and to override limiting beliefs, while priming our brain to see opportunity and align our behaviour towards our desired goals. As you follow this book, you will learn why all of these things are integral to mastering manifestation.

If you want to learn more about the science of manifesting, I suggest checking out Dr Tara Swart's book, *The Source*. Tara is a neuroscientist, fellow manifesting expert and a friend of mine, and in her book she backs up the power of manifesting with cognitive research.

THE UNIVERSE

Whenever I talk about manifesting, I will talk about the universe. For me, it is the universe that holds the power and magic behind manifesting; it holds something greater than our conscious awareness. It is an energetic force that holds within it the infinite abundance of the world.

If, for you, this energetic power is something different, then please feel free to replace 'the universe' with your own interpretation at any time throughout the book.

Now, are you ready to unlock your inner power and live your best life?

MANIFEST WITH ROXIE: THE COMMUNITY

One of the most beautiful and wonderful aspects of all my workshops, webinars and group coaching sessions is the community that is built within them. So many online friendships have been born out of my webinars during the 2020 lockdown, and there are countless WhatsApp groups, with hundreds of men and women who have come together after meeting at my events. In these chat groups they support each other, send one another inspirational content and share self-development resources. I honestly can't describe how happy it makes me to see the community growing in this way.

I know that, as we get older, it is not always easy to meet like-minded people and make new friends which is why I want my platform to really become a space for meeting and connection and encourage everyone on it to do this.

If you want to join the community, come along to one of my webinars or in-person workshops or join the 'Manifest with Roxie' Facebook group. You can also use the hashtag #MANIFESTWITHROXIE to share your stories and post about your progress and your manifesting success stories.

STEP 1

BE CLEAR IN YOUR VISION

*'Everything is created twice,
first in the mind and then in reality.'*

ROBIN SHARMA

The first step of any manifesting journey is to be clear in your vision. To put it simply, you can't get to where you want to go if you don't know where it is you are headed. So, before anything else, you need to have clarity on what you want the universe to provide you with.

I should begin by explaining why knowing exactly what you want, and then **visualizing it**, is so important for manifestation. When we create an experience in our mind, our brain responds as if it is really happening. Neuroscientist Dr Tara Swart explains in *The Source* that 'visualisation works because there is surprisingly little difference to the brain between experiencing an event directly in the outside world and a strongly imagined vision of the same event'. For example, if we visualize ourselves in a stressful scenario, our brain will respond as though it is really happening: our nervous system will prepare for fight or flight and will release the stress hormones cortisol and adrenaline. This will cause our heart to beat faster, our breath to shorten and our blood pressure to rise. By imagining a stressful situation in our minds, we create a literal and physiological stress on our body. If, on the other hand, we imagine ourselves in a serene and peaceful setting, our brain will trigger the nervous system to calm down and encourage the body to relax. The images we form in our mind create a physiological change in our body and therefore have the power to influence the reality we then experience. So, as we visualize ourselves having the things that we desire most, we will create a physiological change that will shift our energetic vibrational frequency and consequently determine what we attract into our lives, by the law of attraction.

Visualization helps us to manifest in another way too: when we start to regularly practise visualizing the things that we want, our brain responds by altering our behaviour patterns and our interpretations of our surroundings in line with the imagined goal. It also becomes more perceptive and open to new opportunities that will align with our visualizations, while filtering out any unwanted information that does not. This means that we can literally prime our brains to drive us towards our desired future.

Visualization is probably the most talked-about manifesting tool in the media. Countless celebrities, athletes and CEOs attribute much of their success to repeatedly visualizing their goals. Swimmer Michael Phelps, who won gold at the Olympics a record-breaking twenty-three times, said he used visualization to prepare for all of his races: he would imagine not only winning, but also things going wrong and seeing himself overcome any challenges with ease. By visually rehearsing all the scenarios and always seeing the best possible outcome, he was able to go into any race totally prepared to win, no matter what.

The more elaborate the visualization, the more real it will feel and the more powerful it becomes. To really bring your visualization to life, try to gain clarity on as many details as you can. **Be as specific as you can when you are designing your dreams.** For example, if you are imagining your dream house, can you specify the location, the number of bedrooms and the layout? Can you see the colour of the front door or picture the flowers in the garden? Think about your visualizations like this: if you were getting in the car to drive to the airport, you wouldn't just type 'airport' into Google Maps and then expect to be led there, would you? No, you would specify the exact airport and the exact terminal you wanted to end up at. Being vague in your visualizations simply won't be enough. The more details you can include and the more specific you are, the clearer you will be in your vision.

The real secret to effective visualization, though, is in understanding that it is not enough to just see the things that you want in your mind. No, to visualize effectively for manifestation, you must immerse yourself in the *feeling* of having them. Remember, **we attract what we feel**. It is only when we can see what we want and then create the emotional experience of having it that we change our vibrational frequency. So, when we imagine our dream home, for example, we must also imagine how it would actually *feel* to live there. The more intensely we can create the feeling of having what we want, the more easily it will come to us. Similarly, if you want to manifest meeting your soulmate, then try to visualize not just your perfect partner but how the relationship will make you feel. Can you conjure up those feelings of unconditional love, safety, warmth and of 'being at home' with someone? Whenever we use our visualizations to create a feeling within us, such as contentment, joy, confidence or love, we raise our vibrational frequency (aka our vibe), which allows us to attract high-vibe abundance back to us.

Some of you reading this may be thinking, 'I actually don't know what I want to manifest, and I am finding it really challenging to visualize something specific that I want.' You may not know what job you want, or where you'd like to be living, or how you want your life to look like one year from now. You may be at a pivotal moment in your life where you are seeking change but you don't know which direction to take. If that's the case, then you're not alone. In fact, many people seem to find the magic of manifesting when they are feeling lost, directionless or stuck in their lives. If this is you, then I encourage you to focus your visualizations solely on how you want to feel. For example, you may want to manifest feeling more confident in yourself, more satisfied, more passionate, more driven, more in love, more at peace. You can absolutely manifest a feeling.

I had a client who I worked with very closely last year. When she first came to me she was truly at her rock bottom. She had tried numerous types of therapy and healing techniques, but none of them seemed to work in helping her to create lasting change. She said to me, 'I know you speak a lot about manifesting. Do you think you could help me to manifest, even if I don't know what I want?' I smiled at her and nodded. I asked her if she would be open to doing a meditation with me. She agreed and I guided her to a place of relaxation then asked her to visualize herself six months on from that moment. I asked her to try to identify how her ideal future self would feel, encouraging her to really embody that feeling. After I'd brought her back to the present moment, she explained that what she wanted, more than anything, was to be able to wake up in the morning feeling energized and hopeful about the day ahead. Like many people who have struggled with their mental or emotional health, that was not something she had felt for a long time. In taking her through this visualization and asking her to imagine how she wanted to feel, I had enabled her to begin her manifesting journey. Within six months, not only was she waking up energized and excited about the day ahead, she had gone on to transform her internal and external world in every way. She was thriving in her work, in her personal relationships and in her relationship with herself, and it all started with one thing: *a feeling*.

When visualizing your ideal future, visualize not just *what* you want to manifest, but **the person that you want to be**. In fact, the question 'Who do I want to become?' might be the most important of the whole manifesting process. When you imagine your future self – the person you want to be tomorrow, next month, next year – ask yourself: how does this version of yourself feel physically, emotionally and energetically? How does this version of you behave day to day? What habits do you commit to? How do you handle stressful situations? What values and beliefs do you hold? What kind of relationships are present in your life, and how do they make you feel? Get crystal clear on the person you want to be and love that person unconditionally from this very moment. Know that **this version of you already exists within you**, dormant, but patiently waiting to be brought to life as you follow the rest of the steps in this book.

> THE GREATEST GIFT THAT MANIFESTING CAN OFFER US IS NOT TO HELP US ATTRACT THINGS FOR US TO POSSESS BUT TO HELP US UNLEASH THE MOST EMPOWERED, AUTHENTIC, SELF-LOVING AND TRULY MAGNIFICENT VERSION OF OURSELVES THAT THERE IS.

Whenever I want to immerse myself into a visualization of my future self, I use meditation: I simply sit in a quiet space and focus my attention on my breath, and on the rise and fall of my belly as I inhale and exhale. As I bring all my awareness to the present moment, I can feel my mind and body begin to relax. Once I am in this relaxed state, I allow my imagination to take myself forward in time and then I begin to create my visualization, filling it with colourful details and conjuring up strong feelings and emotions. I usually sit in my visualization for ten to fifteen minutes and I repeat this two or three times a week.

If you are new to meditation, I suggest that you listen to a guided meditation to help bring you to a relaxed state or to take you through your visualization. There are thousands available online – explore a few to find a narrative voice that you really connect with. I love using YouTube as a resource for visualization meditations. Apps such as Calm and Headspace are also very popular and offer a variety of meditations to help bring you into a relaxed state. Alternatively, you can visit my website, where I have created some specific Manifesting Meditations to help you all with your visualizations. (www.roxienafousi.com).

FAQ:

Q: Can you manifest more than one thing at a time?

A: Yes, yes, yes!! Many of us will have multiple things that we want to manifest at any time and, as long as they are aligned with one another, then you can absolutely manifest them all simultaneously. During a visualization meditation, however, try to connect to just one goal or desired outcome at a time so that you can really sink into each imagined experience.

Once you have an idea of where you want to be, who you want to become, and the things you want to manifest into your life, you can create your **vision board**. A vision board is a visual representation of how you want your life to look. Making a creative vision board allows you to have a clearer overview of all the different things that you want to manifest into your life while also adding another dimension to your visualization.

Note: Whenever you are visualizing the things you want or creating a vision board of your perfect life, make a conscious effort to be completely authentic in what it is *you* want. In other words, it is important that you are not writing down what you *think* you should want, or what someone else wants for you, for example, your parents, teachers or partner. For your vision board to be effective, it must honestly represent the person you truly want to become. You must not compare your manifestation to anyone else's either: you don't have to want to manifest a mansion just because your best friend does. The most important thing to remember, though, is that manifestation is not about just attracting *things* into your life. Rather, it is about empowering yourself to live your best life – and let me remind you that the clichés are very much true: true contentment and joy come not from material possessions but from the relationships around us; from our sense of purpose; and from our ability to live in a way that reflects our most authentic self. So, when you are deciding what you want to manifest, choose the things that will bring you the most fulfilment possible and know that the only person who can decide what that is, is you.

CREATING YOUR VISION BOARD

If you search online, you will find a number of different ways to create a vision board. There is no right or wrong way to do this; you can create a vision board in any way you like, as long as you make something that best helps you visualize the life that you want to manifest.

You can choose to design your own style of vision board or you can follow along with me:

1. Set the scene
Light some candles, play some relaxing music and create a calm and meditative environment. Make your vision-boarding exercise a sacred event for you to enjoy and indulge yourself in.

2. Choose your medium
Take a large sheet of card or paper and choose whether you prefer to write down your goals using different coloured pens (either in bullet points or as a free-flowing description) or

whether you want to use images (draw them yourself or cut out pictures or words from magazines or newspapers that reflect the things you want to draw into your life).

Choose whatever feels best for you – just remember to have fun with it.

3. Choose your timeline

At the top of the page, write the exact date by which you want to manifest what's on your vision board.

You could choose to do a six-month, one-year or even a five-year vision board. Personally, I like to do all three.

I sometimes find that people can struggle to know, and visualize, what they want their life to look like one year ahead yet they may feel much more able to visualize their life in five years' time, or vice versa. So, if you are feeling a little stuck, remember: you can always choose a different timeline.

4. Get in the zone

Before you start adding things to your board, make sure you are already embodying the feeling of your future self. Pause for a moment, take a few deep breaths and imagine yourself exactly six months, or one year or five years from now. Create a clear and vivid image in your mind as you ask yourself the following questions:

- How do I feel within myself?
- What kind of relationships surround me?
- What kind of home do I live in?
- What is my profession?
- What am I most proud of?
- What do I want to change in my life?
- What do I want to keep the same?

As you answer these questions, allow yourself to be completely free in your dreams, desires and wants. Do not allow fear to hold back your imagination; instead, take your mind's eye to the exact place that you want to be. Allow the image of your future self to really come to life as you sink into that visualization.

5. Separate your life into categories[1]
Split your vision board into six categories:

- Personal development (i.e. your personal growth/how you want to feel within yourself)
- Love and romance
- Career
- Friends and family
- House/home
- Hobbies/leisure

6. Design your life
For each category, write down all the things that you want to manifest within it. If you are using cut-out images, such as an image of your dream house, stick them on to your vision board.

I would try to have a minimum of three things for each category. but there is no limit on how many things you can add to your vision board.

7. Put it away
After creating your vision board, put it away somewhere safe and set a reminder to come back to it on the date you wrote at the top.

---

1   This step is optional. I personally love to do this, because it helps me clarify what I want in all areas of my life, rather than focusing in on just one part.

As the things on your vision board begin to manifest into your life and you begin to embody the person you have always wanted to be, your desires or goals may change or expand. As you grow, your dreams will grow, too. Go with the flow of it and be totally flexible with your visualizations. If you want to go back and add something to your vision board, or take something away, feel free to go and do that.

Remember: you are the designer, curator and architect of your life and you always have the power to rearrange, alter and dictate how you want it to look.

Knowing what you want is the first step of any manifesting process. But before I take you on to the next steps, there is something I want you to remember:

To truly understand who we want to become and to begin that journey towards meeting our most empowered selves, **we must first let go of the person we once were and the person we thought we should be**. Our past is equally as responsible for getting us to where we are today as it is for holding us back from where we want to go. Many of us hold a subconscious assumption that we are unchangeable. How many times have you heard, or said, that phrase, 'A leopard never changes its spots?' This proverb literally tells us that it is impossible for someone to change. Or how many times have you said something along the lines of 'I've just always been that way,' or 'That's just who I am?' While they might just seem like harmless expressions, they support an underlying belief that only one version of us can ever exist. This creates a lack of trust in our ability to transform, evolve and grow, which serves only to hold us back from doing so. But change is not only possible, it is inevitable. The person you were yesterday is not the person you are today or the person you will be tomorrow. So, as you go forward on your manifesting journey, throughout this book and beyond, I encourage you all to honour your daily transformation.

With each new day, honour who you are and the person that you want to become without being constrained by your past. It's OK to feel differently, it's OK to want something different and it's OK to become someone new. Lean into it and allow the magic of manifesting to propel you into becoming your highest self.

WITH EACH SUNRISE, WE RISE INTO SOMEONE NEW.

As you embark on your manifesting journey, take time to really consider what exactly you want the universe to bring to you, connecting to *why* you want it and how it will make you feel to have it. Be as specific as you can with your dreams, and if you can't yet visualize a 'thing', then re-create a feeling. Practise regularly sinking into a visualization of your future self, allowing the feeling of it to change your vibe instantly, while simultaneously directing your brain to begin driving you towards reaching that goal. Then have fun with your dreams: create a vision board that represents your best life and allow it to become your reality as you continue uncovering my 7-step guide to manifesting.

STEP 2

REMOVE FEAR AND DOUBT

*'Fear and self-doubt have always been
the greatest enemies of human potential.'*

BRIAN TRACY

The most important thing to understand about manifesting is this: you do not manifest from your conscious thoughts alone. You manifest from your **subconscious** beliefs about what you deserve. This means that **you can only manifest what you _truly_ believe you are worthy of attracting into your life.**

According to research, only 5 per cent of our cognitive activity is conscious, while the remaining 95 per cent is subconscious. That means that 95 per cent of our thoughts, reactions, decisions, perceptions and behavioural patterns are driven by the subconscious parts of our brains. When you consider this, it is easy to understand why our subconscious would then have such a profound influence over the reality we create. But while our subconscious has unlimited power to drive us _towards_ our dreams, it also has the power to _hold us back_ from them. This is because our subconscious is home to the two things that block any manifestation: _fear and doubt._

Fear and doubt come in the form of insecurities, limiting beliefs, feelings of unworthiness and a lack of trust in the universe's ability to provide for us. Fear and doubt sabotage our manifesting abilities by subconsciously sending a message to the universe that we aren't worthy enough, or ready, to receive the things that we desire.

Fear and doubt are so powerful that they can prevent us from even *imagining* what we want: they literally create blocks for us at the very first step of our manifesting journey. Let me show you how: I would like you to take a minute to pause and visualize the exact income you wish to manifest in the next financial year. Write down the figure on a piece of paper now. When you look at this figure, can you honestly say that this is your *dream* salary? Or did you write down a figure you believed you could 'realistically' manifest?

> FEAR AND DOUBT OFTEN MASK
> THEMSELVES AS FRIENDS; THEY TELL
> YOU THEY'RE PROTECTING YOU
> FROM INEVITABLE DISAPPOINTMENT,
> WHEN IN REALITY THEY ARE
> ACTIVELY HOLDING YOU BACK FROM
> UNLOCKING THE ABUNDANCE OF
> THE UNIVERSE.

Ask yourself now: when making your vision board in the previous step, did you stop yourself writing down some of your deepest desires because something within you told you that they're unachievable and there was no point in adding them in? Your limiting beliefs can prevent you from even visualizing what you want from life by telling you that your dreams are simply out of the realm of possibility.

A couple of months ago my best friend, Leah, came over because she wanted me to help her begin her manifesting journey. We lit candles, set the scene and I took her through a visualization meditation, then we laid out large sheets of coloured paper, magazines and marker pens and got started on making our vision boards. I could see her hesitating every few minutes, going to write something then stopping herself. I paused and asked her, 'What are you not writing down?' and she replied, 'I just want to be realistic.' When we shared our vision boards with each other after we had finished, I saw that she had crossed out '10 new clients' and replaced it with '5 new clients'. When I asked her why she had done that she said it was because she didn't want to put something down 'in case it didn't happen'. As she is my best friend and we talk endlessly about the things we want to achieve in our lives and the dreams we have, I could see that she had also completely avoided writing down some of her deepest desires. One thing was for sure: fear and doubt had a hold of her.

I did the very same thing at the beginning of my own manifesting journey. It was New Year's Eve and, unlike the previous ten years, I decided *not* to spend the night getting drunk and then struggle through the first day of the new year with a raging hangover, but instead to spend the evening at home, cooking my favourite meal and sitting down to make my vision boards – something that has now become my New Year's Eve ritual. I had just begun creating my first-ever five-year vision board and I could feel so much resistance and self-doubt coming up as I was doing it. For example, I dreamed of being on stage delivering one of my self-development workshops to thousands of people. The reason for this? I want to empower as many people as I can to realize and see the infinite power they have within them to heal, evolve and live the very best version of their lives. I want to contribute, in any way I can, towards making self-development as fashionable and mainstream as clothes are. That's my purpose, my passion and my goal. When it came to it, though, I couldn't bring myself to put it on my vision board. I was so embarrassed by the thought of writing it down and it not coming true that I denied myself the opportunity to even consider it was possible. My fear was trying to protect me from the threat of failure, but it was also preventing me from manifesting something I wanted.

I realized that creating a vision board can do more than simply help you visualize what you want to manifest: it can give you an opportunity to understand your fears and doubts more clearly. Every time you hold yourself back from writing something on your vision board, ask yourself, 'Why am I holding back? What limiting belief is driving that?' By identifying your fears and doubts at this stage, you give yourself an opportunity to start to work on healing and removing them so that you can unblock your path to manifesting everything and anything that you want.

When I came to create my next vision board, I challenged myself to write down every single dream I had, no matter how big or small, and I refused to let my insecurities stop me from doing so.

WHEN WE GIVE OURSELVES FULL PERMISSION TO DREAM, OUR FEARS AND DOUBTS HAVE NOWHERE TO HIDE.

Try this: If your previous vision board was limited by fear and doubt, go back and amend it now, or create a brand-new one that honestly represents all the things you *really* want. Before you do this, say to yourself, 'If fear and doubt were no object, this is what I would like to manifest into my life.' Put down every single thing that you want to attract.

Dream big and don't hold back.

TO MANIFEST *ANYTHING* INTO YOUR LIFE, AND TO DO SO EFFORTLESSLY AND EFFECTIVELY, YOU *MUST* BELIEVE YOU ARE WORTHY OF HAVING IT. *READ THAT AGAIN.*

For example, let's imagine that you are an artist and you want to manifest successfully selling your artwork. You can visualize yourself displaying your art at a gallery you love, and you can imagine exactly how it will feel to sell your work, but if you don't, deep down, believe that you are good enough or worthy of praise and celebration, then you will not be able to attract the opportunities for your work to be appreciated. We attract not just what we feel, but what we believe. **You simply cannot manifest when fear and doubt stand in your way.** So, to progress in any manifesting journey you must first identify and then work to remove the fear and doubt roadblocks. This is what I call *inner work*. This is *self-development in action*. At this point, it is important to acknowledge that the inner work required to remove our fear and doubt is ongoing. Some of your limiting beliefs may be relatively easy to observe and let go of, while others may be more deep-rooted and require a great deal of attention, time and commitment to work through so that they no longer have the power to limit you.

The majority of us have an endless list of limiting beliefs, insecurities and doubts that we have accumulated from our early childhoods through to where we are now. They plague our conscious and subconscious minds and block us from unlocking our greatest potential. This is why Step 2 on my 7-step guide to manifesting is one that you will keep coming back to again and again throughout your manifesting journey.

FAQ:

Q: What is a limiting belief?

A: A belief is formed when a thought has been repeated so many times that it has become automatic. Our beliefs drive our behaviour, so when a belief that we have is holding us back in some way, it becomes a limiting belief.

For example, if we grew up being told over and over again that we are unlovable, we will eventually believe it to be true and the way we behave will be informed by that belief system. This may mean that, later in life, we will accept being treated poorly by others or we will subconsciously seek out toxic relationships to support this self-limiting belief.

Beliefs can be formed in childhood, adolescence and in adulthood.

Before I go on, I would like to tell you a little story about my own relationship with fear and doubt.

When I look back at my life before I discovered manifesting, I was drowning in insecurity. My self-loathing was debilitating and my lack of self-worth impacted on every area of my life. I was conscious of it at the time (my inner critic was far too loud to ever be ignored), but it all stemmed from a place deep within me: from my past experiences and from memories that lived within my subconscious. My own journey to removing fear and doubt was the most valuable and profound I have ever been on. It is a journey that is still ongoing, and I continue to work on this step every day. I have become acutely aware of my thoughts, and when fear and doubt begin to speak I take a moment to catch them, consider where they are coming from and then take immediate action to heal them, using some of the tools I'm going to take you through in a moment.

One of the (many) limiting beliefs I held was this: I would never be successful in my own right. Growing up, I had always wanted to ensure that I would have financial stability in my life. Like many people, I wanted to feel comfortable in a home that I loved, and I didn't want to have to worry about paying bills or providing for my children. But I grew up believing that in order for that to happen I would need a husband who could provide that for me. I told myself that I wasn't capable enough, or intelligent enough, to become a successful and financially independent woman in my own right. Then, at the age of twenty-one, I fell madly, deeply, head over heels in love with someone twenty-five years older than me. I was completely besotted with him, and the two years we were together felt, at the time, like a fairy tale. He made me feel so safe and adored, and he imparted so much wisdom to me and taught me so much, which shaped the person I have become today. But he was also an incredibly successful, wealthy man and he provided me with a certain lifestyle that I would not otherwise have experienced at that point in my life. This reaffirmed my limiting belief that I needed someone else to support me. I began to place all my value and self-worth in him and, when the relationship ended abruptly, I was devastatingly heartbroken and suffered a complete loss of identity. In truth, before I discovered manifesting, I used *all* my romantic relationships to make myself feel validated. In my mind, I was only ever as good as the man I was with and my self-worth was always directly related to the person I fell asleep beside.

At the time, I was totally unaware that I was stuck in this pattern but, unsurprisingly, in all those years I made virtually no money myself. I was unable to secure jobs, and I had no direction, purpose or motivation. My own fears and doubts prevented me from manifesting any work or financial independence and from stepping into my own light.

Shortly after I did discover manifesting, as I described earlier, I met Wade, the father of my child and now best friend. This time, I had met someone who was my equal and not someone I looked to for validation or someone who would enable me to escape my own world by bringing me into theirs. Instead, Wade offered me something so much more magical: unparalleled emotional support, unconditional love and the freedom to be completely and utterly myself. I believe that meeting Wade was one of the best things that ever happened to me, not just because of our beautiful son, but because I don't think I would have been so driven and focused on building my own career to the place it is now without him by my side helping me to see that *I was enough*.

As I began to manifest more and more, I finally realized that I was completely able to provide myself with all the financial stability and validation that I dreamed of. I didn't need anyone else to provide it for me. I knew that the only things that had ever held me back from having it were fear and doubt. Fear that I wasn't smart enough, worthy enough or good enough, and a subconscious doubt, influenced by both my upbringing and the media, that it was possible for a woman to carve out a successful career for herself. I worked through each fear and doubt and committed to healing it. Between 2018 and 2020, my income increased tenfold. Now, as I write this, I am proud to say that I have provided myself with all the financial stability I dreamed of as a child. I can take my son on holiday, I can pay my bills without worrying and I can spoil the people I love most. The power was always within me, I just had to unlock it first.

IDENTIFY FEAR AND DOUBT

When you look at all the things that you want to attract into your life, you must first commit to being open and honest with yourself in order to recognize what fears and doubts you currently have about being able to manifest them.

Start by asking yourself some questions:

- ○ Do I really believe I am worthy of it?
- ○ Do I really trust that I would be able to handle it?
- ○ Do I really believe it is possible for me?
- ○ What insecurities do I currently have surrounding this?
- ○ What limiting beliefs are holding me back?

I invite you now to take a moment to think about just one thing that you want to manifest. See it clearly in your mind's eye and then spend a few minutes trying to identify what fears and doubts come into your mind when you think about really having it. Try to identify as many as you can and write them down in the space below.

> **Note:** However quiet the inner voice is that keeps you from fully believing in yourself, bring it to light and write it down. Even if your thoughts feel irrational or unreasonable, write them down. Acknowledging each detail of your fear and doubt will only empower you to let it go.

What do I want to manifest?

....
....
....
....
....
....

What fears and doubts do I have around this?

. . . .
. . . .
. . . .
. . . .
. . . .
. . . .

Take a look at the fears and doubts you have just identified and understand this: **it is these limiting beliefs and insecurities that are currently holding you back from living your best life**. The more aware you become of them, the less power they hold over you. Awareness is always the starting point for any self-development journey. Simply by completing that exercise and identifying your limiting beliefs, you have already begun the process of healing them.

I suggest that you repeat this exercise for every single thing that you want to manifest, or at any point when you feel stuck in your manifestation to help you recognize your current blocks. Become a mindful observer of your day-to-day thoughts and when the voices of insecurity begin to speak, take note. The more easily you are able to identify them, the more quickly you will be able to let them go.

REMOVE FEAR AND DOUBT

Removing fear and doubt is self-development in action. This is the work we commit to every single day: to remove limiting beliefs, to realize our worth, to unlock our potential and to rediscover the inner confidence we were born with. This is the inner work we commit to so that we can successfully manifest the life of our dreams. This is the work we do so that we can live a life that is not limited by our own insecurities but flourishes with the power of the universe.

So how do we do it? There are endless ways that we can begin to heal fear and doubt, but here are four I've found particularly powerful that I want to share with you:

1. Master your thoughts
2. Watch your language
3. Use mantras
4. Practise visualization

Note: For some of you reading this, your fear and doubt may have stemmed from trauma or it may feel too overwhelming to begin to work through it alone. If this is the case, working with a therapist, holistic healer, psychiatrist, counsellor or other mental health professional can be a necessary and valuable investment to help you heal and work towards removing the fear and doubt, alongside the suggestions below.

1. Master your thoughts

I began this chapter with an important lesson: we do not manifest from our conscious thoughts alone but from our subconscious beliefs about what we deserve. While this is true, we must not underestimate the power of our thoughts and the influence they continuously have over our subconscious.

> THE SUBCONSCIOUS MIND OBEYS
> THE CONSCIOUS MIND, SO
> WHATEVER WE CONSCIOUSLY THINK
> OUR SUBCONSCIOUS WILL PERCEIVE
> TO BE TRUE.

How do you talk about yourself to yourself? Most of us have a voice inside our head that will speak to us in pretty unkind ways. It will tell us we are unworthy, unlovable, stupid, disgusting, boring and any other disempowering characteristics it can think of. This voice is the expression of our fears and doubts. In my webinars, I do an exercise where I ask everyone to say something kind to themselves; for example, I will encourage them to repeat, inside their heads or out loud, 'I am wonderful, I am beautiful, the people in my life are so lucky to have me, I am perfect exactly as I am, I love myself.' Afterwards, I ask them to tell me how it felt to do that. Every time, the majority will say that they felt silly and uncomfortable speaking to themselves in that way, even when no one else could hear them. I then ask them to say something like 'I am worthless, I am never enough,' and ask them how that felt. Too easy, they tell me. I do this short exercise to demonstrate just how natural and effortless it feels for us to speak to ourselves in limiting ways, and how unnatural and challenging it feels to speak to ourselves with love and respect.

I can relate to them; I spent two decades looking in the mirror saying things like 'You're hideous, you're a loser, you're miserable, you'll never be enough.' I spent every single day berating myself for simply being me, and my inner voice was constantly feeding my devastatingly low self-esteem. *I gave my insecurity a voice, and with that voice it grew.* There came a point, though, when I was simply exhausted by it all and I just didn't have the energy to inflict that verbal abuse on myself any longer. Perhaps some of you reading this now are feeling exactly like that, too. I realized that I was never going to be able to step into my fullest power and unlock the life of my dreams if I continued speaking to myself in this way.

I made a choice to start showing up for myself and to become my own cheerleader. I did it even though it didn't feel comfortable. I said kind and loving things to myself because I knew my subconscious would hear it and believe it to be true, even if I didn't. Once I started to choose thoughts that supported me and empowered me, I began to feel an internal shift in my confidence. If I could sense I was about to voice something negative or limiting, I would catch myself and instead say something like 'You are doing a great job. You can achieve anything you put your mind to. You are strong. You can do this. It's OK.' I knew that every time I used the power of my thoughts in this way I was boosting my manifesting power. Within a month, I noticed that this was beginning to feel natural, and within two months it had become the leading inner voice. I really started to believe the things I was saying, and I meant it when I said to myself, 'You got this!' or 'You should be so proud of yourself.' I mastered my thoughts to override the fear and doubt. I urge you all to become your own cheerleaders, too.

IF WE KNOW THAT OUR SUBCONSCIOUS IS DRIVING US TO OUR MANIFESTATION, THEN WE MUST USE OUR CONSCIOUS MINDS TO INFLUENCE OUR SUBCONSCIOUS BELIEFS. WE MUST FEED OUR SUBCONSCIOUS WITH EMPOWERING THOUGHTS TO INCREASE OUR SELF-WORTH AND BOOST OUR MANIFESTING POWER.

Our thoughts shape our reality in another way, too. Remember, in the introduction, I explained that thoughts generate emotions and that different emotions have different vibrational frequencies. This means that if we can master our thoughts, we can change our emotional state, and if we change our emotional state, we can change our vibration. If we change our vibration, we change our reality.

So, when we consciously choose to think positive and empowering thoughts that trigger high-vibe emotions (such as confidence, enthusiasm and hope), we will attract more abundance into our lives through the law of attraction. However, if we allow fear and doubt to express themselves continuously as a negative voice or an inner critic, they will lower our self-worth, trigger low-vibe emotions (such as fear, shame, despair or worry) and block our manifestations.

We can only have one thought at a time. I remember hearing that for the first time and wondering why something so obvious had never occurred to me before. If we can only have one thought at a time, then, surely, we can just *choose* to replace a negative thought with a positive one, right? The answer is yes.

But we are creatures of habit not just in what we do but also in the way that we think. The National Science Foundation, an independent health agency based in the US, found that we have, on average, up to 60,000 thoughts a day. Of those, approximately 80 per cent are negative and over 90 per cent are repetitive. To begin to undo repetitive, negative and limiting ways of thinking, we must *commit* to consistent practice and repeatedly **choose to nourish our mind by replacing the negative thoughts with empowering ones**. Commit to it in just the same way you would commit to forming any other new habit.

Each time you find yourself thinking, 'What if it doesn't work out?', ask yourself, 'What if it does?' Instead of saying, 'I'm not good enough,' say, 'I am perfect exactly as I am.' Instead of imagining the worst possible outcome, imagine the best. Remember that you have the gift of choice, so choose a thought that pushes you forward rather than one that holds you back.

DO NOT ALLOW NEGATIVE THOUGHTS TO ROAM FREE, UNREGULATED AND UNMANAGED. TAKE OWNERSHIP OF THEM AND START TO PRACTISE MANAGING YOUR THOUGHTS SO THAT THEY CAN WORK FOR YOU, RATHER THAN AGAINST YOU.

As well as replacing thoughts, we can also work towards removing our fear and doubt by **reframing our perspective**.

No matter what we experience, we always have an opportunity to choose which lens we view it through. The perspective we tend to choose is usually dictated by our general mood, our expectations, our past experiences, our belief systems and our self-worth. This is why two people can experience the exact same situation but perceive it in very different ways. For example, have you ever been at a restaurant with a friend and when you leave one of you says that it was a perfect evening, while the other felt the restaurant was too loud, the food was average and the staff were inattentive? Or have you ever read an email from a colleague when you were in a bad mood and felt personally attacked and completely infuriated by them, only to re-read it the next day and realize that you had totally misinterpreted their tone?

Our perspective is informed by many external factors, but we always have the power to choose one that will serve us best. In fact, reframing my perspective is the technique I use most frequently to overcome any fear or doubt that creeps in throughout the day. Whenever I sense myself starting to worry or doubt something, I pause and see if I could offer myself a new perspective. For example, I called my sister just last week to tell her how disappointed and upset I was that an article I had written had not been published. My inner critic was trying to convince me that it was because my work wasn't good enough and that the editor had decided she didn't want me writing for their publication any more. After voicing this out loud, I remembered that I had the opportunity to choose a different perspective. Instead, I chose to focus my thoughts on how proud I was to have written the article and how grateful I was to be asked at all. I came up with three alternative scenarios as to why the article had not yet been published, none of which had anything to do with me: the editor hadn't seen the email; they had other articles they needed to publish first; they had decided to take a different direction with the piece. In a matter of minutes, I moved away from my negative perspective and embraced a more liberating one. My article was published the very next morning.

When you see that you are interpreting a situation from a place of fear and doubt, ask yourself, 'What is another perspective I could choose? How could I reframe my thinking here?'

For example, if you go on a date with someone and the next day you don't hear from them, you have a choice of what perspective you can take. If you allow your fear and doubt to dictate your perspective, you might start to question what you did or said wrong, you might decide that this is further evidence that you will never meet the right person for you and you may allow it to stop you from opening yourself up to future dating opportunities out of fear of feeling rejected again. However, if you adopt a more empowering perspective, you might choose to consider that perhaps the other person is not in a place in their lives to meet someone right now, that the two of you just weren't the right fit, and you would still feel excited about the journey to meeting your soulmate.

REMEMBER: WE MANIFEST WHAT WE BELIEVE WE ARE WORTHY OF.

Start to become aware of your thoughts, then choose to replace those expressions of fear and doubt with thoughts and perspectives that will raise your self-worth and self-belief.

2. Watch your language
The language we use both internally and aloud feeds directly into our subconscious. As with our thoughts, if the language we use is unregulated, it will work against us by fuelling our fears and doubts.

There are a few easy ways to use language to help you manifest more effectively:

Remove the word 'if' and replace it with 'when'

When people talk about the things they want to manifest or the goals they want to reach, they often use the word 'if', for example, 'If I get that job . . .' or 'If I meet someone . . .' The word 'if' says to the universe, 'I don't really know, or trust, that this will actually happen.' **The doubt is highlighted in the 'if', and you cannot manifest from a place of doubt.** From now on, I ask that you never use the word 'if' again. Instead, say 'when', for example, 'When I get my new job . . .' or 'When I meet my perfect partner . . .' When you talk about your future using language that reflects certainty, your subconscious will respond by directing everything towards you reaching that goal.

Talk about what you *do* want, not what you don't

If you were to tell me now about something that you really don't want to happen, you would have to first imagine what it would feel like if it *did* happen. So, when we speak about something we don't want, our subconscious still mentally and emotionally experiences it. As we now know, this will change our vibration to that of the imagined, unwanted experience and that is what we will then attract. So, the more we discuss what we don't want, the more it will show up for us.

Instead, simply describe what you *do* want. For example, instead of saying, 'I really don't want to be in debt any more,' say, 'I want financial freedom.' Or, instead of saying, 'I hate being single,' say 'I am excited to be in a healthy, loving relationship when the time is right.'

Use your awareness to ensure that rather than expressing what you fear might happen or hope won't happen, you focus your energy on the things you *do* want in your life so that you can bring them into your reality.

Make mindful swaps

There is language that empowers us, and there is language that limits us. And the language we use matters. When we become more aware of the language we are using, we can implement some simple yet effective language swaps to help boost our manifesting power. For example, every time you find yourself saying, 'I can't do this,' or 'It's too hard,' you might choose, instead, to say, 'I will find a way to do this.' **Remember that your subconscious mind, the place that you manifest from, is obeying your conscious mind and listening to the language that you use.**

I had a client who really struggled with public speaking. He said that every week, when the team meeting began on Monday morning, his palms would get sweaty and he would feel hot and flustered at the thought of having to give his pitch. It was interfering with his weekends because the anticipation of it was becoming so overwhelming. Within our conversations he kept using phrases such as 'I hate public speaking,' or 'I am so inarticulate,' or 'I am rubbish in team meetings.' He was feeding his fears with this limiting language, but this way of speaking had become so automatic that he wasn't even aware of it. I encouraged him to spend the next week becoming conscious of whenever he was about to use one of these phrases, and instead say to himself, 'I love being able to share my ideas with others,' or 'I am grateful to be part of a team who listen to what I have to say,' or 'I am a really confident speaker.' I reminded him that it was OK if it felt a little uncomfortable to say these things, but to really commit to doing it anyway. When the next Monday team meeting came around, he told me that although his voice was shaking for the first few seconds, he managed to finish his pitch without stumbling over his words the way he usually did. I could see how proud he was of himself as he told me the story, and I felt so proud of him, too. The following week, he did it again, and the week after that he told me, in his own words, that he was so looking forward to the meeting on Monday to share something new with the team. By changing the language he used he was able to override his fear and doubt and increase his self-esteem surrounding public speaking.

When we change our language, we change our experiences.

Here are some examples of simple language swaps that you can use:

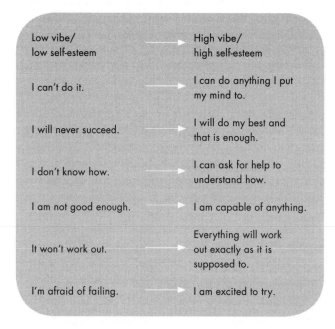

Low vibe/ low self-esteem	High vibe/ high self-esteem
I can't do it.	I can do anything I put my mind to.
I will never succeed.	I will do my best and that is enough.
I don't know how.	I can ask for help to understand how.
I am not good enough.	I am capable of anything.
It won't work out.	Everything will work out exactly as it is supposed to.
I'm afraid of failing.	I am excited to try.

Become aware of the language you use and make mindful swaps wherever possible to keep feeding your subconscious with nourishing thoughts that will boost your self-worth, self-belief and ability to attract abundance into your life.

Accept compliments
Many of us grew up believing that speaking confidently about ourselves would make us seem arrogant, vain or boastful. So,

we embraced the use of self-deprecating language and learned to put ourselves down in an attempt to be more likeable. Take a second to think about all the times someone has paid you a compliment or congratulated you on your achievements: how many times did you respond with denial, objection or by playing down your success?

This has become such a natural way to respond to compliments, but it is doing more damage to your self-esteem than you might think. When a friend says to you, 'Wow, you look really glowing and radiant today,' and you respond with 'Urgh, no, I look awful,' you send a message to your subconscious that you do indeed look awful.

Little by little, as we dismiss and reject the compliments and praise we receive from others, we subtly chip away at our own self-worth. From now, commit to practising a greater level of openness and gratitude when someone pays you a compliment. Take a moment to really hear what they have said and respond instead with nothing but those two magical words: 'Thank you.'

When we open ourselves up to receiving expressions of love or praise from other people, we simultaneously begin to shift our subconscious beliefs about what we deserve. This is such a simple and effective change to make, and it's one that I absolutely love.

3. Use mantras

A mantra is a word, phrase or sound that you can repeat out loud or in your head at any time, to help gain awareness, release stress and to raise your vibration.

When I discuss the use of mantras in the context of manifesting, I am referring to using a positive affirming phrase such as 'I am worthy.'

We can use mantras to send positive messages to our subconscious minds and to replace a negative thought. For example, if your fear and doubt was beginning to voice itself as something like 'You are not good enough,' you can replace the thought with a mantra such as 'I am perfect exactly as I am.'

When we begin to incorporate mantras into our daily routine, for example by repeating them every morning or every night before bed, we can begin to reprogramme our subconscious mind by regularly feeding it with positive and empowering language.

Mantras are one of my all-time favourite self-development tools and incorporating them into my life has been an integral part of my own manifesting journey. Whenever I repeat a mantra out loud or inside my head I instantly feel more centred and empowered. When I first started using mantras, though, I found the experience really confronting. I felt both silly and embarrassed to be saying to myself, 'I am worthy,' when, at that time, I didn't feel worthy at all. But I committed to the practice anyway because I knew that it was shifting something at a deeper level, the subconscious level, the level from which we manifest. Within a couple of days of repeating these affirming statements every morning when I woke up, I was finding myself saying them more easily and without that awkward and uncomfortable feeling. Within a week, I was really able to focus my attention on the words I was saying and feel my whole energy shift with it. Now, I never go a day without repeating a mantra to myself. I always repeat a couple of mantras to myself in the morning to start my day in the best possible way, and any time I need an energetic boost, too.

Try this: Write down a mantra somewhere you will see it every day, for example, as your phone screensaver or a note on your bathroom mirror. Whenever you see it, repeat it to yourself five times. I like to change my mantra once a week so that I give each one enough time to really let the message sink into my subconscious.

Here are some mantra ideas to get you started. Choose one or two a week and repeat it five times every morning and every evening. As you read them now, repeat them to yourself slowly a couple of times and see for yourself just how quickly you can shift your energy.

- ○ I love the person that I am today.
- ○ I have limitless potential.
- ○ I am grateful for all that I have.
- ○ I love my life.
- ○ I feel calm and at peace.
- ○ I radiate vitality and energy.
- ○ I have infinite power to manifest anything I desire.
- ○ I am consistently attracting abundance into my life.

One way that we can use mantras to reprogramme our subconscious beliefs is to listen to a **positive affirmations track**. A positive affirmations track is an extended audio track that repeats a number of mantras in a loop, usually over meditative music. I recommend this tool to absolutely everyone I work with because affirmations are so powerful and so effective in helping us with our manifesting journeys.

How do they work? Well, our subconscious is most susceptible to positive messaging at three significant points of the day: as we fall asleep, as we wake up and when we are in a meditative state. This is because at these times our brain is operating between the frequencies of alpha and theta brain waves, the optimum frequency for visualization, creativity and learning. Listening to a positive affirmations track at these specific times will allow your subconscious to most effectively absorb the positive messaging, and when you do this repeatedly, it forms new neural pathways in the brain that support a more empowered, and therefore magnetic, mindset. It will also help to overwrite any negative and limiting beliefs driven by fear and doubt.

I began using positive affirmations at the very beginning of my manifesting journey, listening to them as I was falling asleep, and I still, three years on, fall asleep to them every single night. I first listened to tracks that I found on YouTube; I just typed in 'affirmation tracks' and chose the one that I connected with most. Now, though, I use tracks that I created myself, which are all available on my website (www.roxienafousi.com). Once you find one you like, I recommend sticking with it for a while: our minds become conditioned to a particular track, so as soon as you press play your brain will know that now it's time to relax and you can sink more quickly into that susceptible, meditative state.

If you are working towards manifesting a specific goal, then I suggest listening to an affirmations track focused around that goal. For example, if you are wanting to manifest a promotion, then I suggest listening to a career-focused affirmations track every night for two weeks. Similarly, if you are wanting to manifest your soulmate, then perhaps choose a self-love or relationships-focused affirmation track.

4. Practise visualization
We used visualization in Step 1: Be Clear in Your Vision (see page 9), and we can use it again now as a tool to help us remove fear and doubt.

Here is a simple visualization for you to try:

THE EVAPORATING BALL VISUALIZATION

Close your eyes and take a deep inhalation and a full exhalation, noticing the rise and fall of your belly. Inhale for the count of four and exhale for the count of four. Repeat this deep breathing until you notice that your mind is beginning to quieten and your body to relax. Once you have reached a place of relaxation, use your mind's eye to visualize your fear and doubt. See all the fear-driven thoughts, feelings and emotions collected together as a ball of dark matter. Imagine all your insecurities, worries and limiting beliefs joining it, making this ball bigger and bigger. See it clearly in front of you, a representation of everything that is holding you back from your fullest power. Now, with each *inhalation*, imagine a bright line shining through you, overpowering the darkness. With each *exhalation*, visualize this ball of fear getting smaller and smaller. Repeat this until the ball of dark matter, the ball of fear and doubt, has evaporated into nothing. Then, gently, open your eyes.

I love this visualization technique because you can use it any time and anywhere. Even if a little niggle of doubt comes into your mind, you can simply close your eyes and imagine yourself removing it with the power of your breath.

This technique is particularly useful for anyone who feels exceptionally overwhelmed by their inner voice and finds mastering their thoughts, or using mantras, to be too overwhelming to begin with. I had one client who was newly married and was really struggling to find her voice in her relationship. She felt constantly undervalued and unappreciated and felt that she wasn't getting the emotional support she needed. Even though she knew this, her inner critic was so loud that it stopped her from being able to communicate what she needed and deserved from her partner and it was taking a toll on her mental health. She came to me for help with releasing some of her limiting beliefs surrounding love and relationships and with making her feel more confident within her marriage. But I could see, soon into our first session, that her inner critic was so overbearing that asking her to replace her limiting thoughts with empowering ones was going to feel really daunting and unmanageable for her. So instead I asked her to try this visualization technique and to repeat it every day for two weeks. By the end of the fourteen days she had managed to take enough power away from the fear and doubt to be able to start incorporating some of the other tools, too, such as using mantras and switching her language. Within six weeks, she had begun to find, and use, her voice; she was finally communicating her needs to her partner in a healthy way and was feeling much more empowered within herself and in her relationship.

We can use visualization to remove fear and doubt in another way, too. Just as we can use our thoughts to reframe our perspectives, we can use visualization to reimagine the scenarios we play in our minds. How often do you find yourself playing out worst-case scenarios in your head? Or imagining your worst fears coming true? When we repeatedly play out these scenes in our minds, we lower our vibe and feed into our worries, insecurities and doubts. You can use the power of visualization to simply reimagine the scenes you are watching in your mind and choose to see the best possible outcome playing out instead; it's a bit like changing the channel on TV. For example, let's say you want to manifest getting into your dream university, if your fear and doubt is creating scenarios in your mind of you failing the exams you need to pass to get in or receiving a letter with bad news, then change the channel. Visualize yourself passing the exam and receiving the good news you've been waiting for and really imagine how you will feel in that moment. Keep replaying the ideal outcome in your head over and over again.

Visualizations are a firm fixture in your manifesting toolbox; you can use them to be clear in your vision, to help remove fear and doubt, to imagine yourself in best-case scenarios and to raise your vibe.

> OUR MINDS HAVE INCREDIBLE POWER; THEY ARE BOTH THE CAUSE AND THE CURE OF OUR FEAR AND DOUBT.

Fear and doubt are the words I use to describe the culmination of everything that feeds into our low self-worth, our insecurities and the limiting beliefs that block us from turning our dreams into reality. As I mentioned earlier, removing your fear and doubt is an ongoing process, and it is the one that I always remind people to keep coming back to. When you find yourself blocked on any manifestation, the first thing to do is ask yourself what fears and doubts are still surrounding your ability to call it in. It is worth me adding here that this is probably the most challenging step of all: it requires us to be vulnerable and to look back at all the experiences and memories that may have contributed to creating these blocks in the first place. But with great effort comes great reward and, once you have begun to remove these blocks, you will clear the pathway to receiving the infinite abundance that the universe is waiting to provide you with. The four tools in this chapter are just some of the tools you can use day to day, but I encourage you to explore any other self-development practices that help you on your journey to raising your self-worth.

We are now going to move on to perhaps the most powerful way that we can combat fear and doubt; it is something that will permeate each and every step in the manifesting process: cultivating self-love.

CULTIVATE AND PRACTISE SELF-LOVE

When I began writing this book, I kept trying to figure out where I should speak about self-love. It isn't a step in itself, but whenever I tried to fit it into one of the other steps, I couldn't help but feel that I wasn't giving it the attention it deserved. I realized that self-love needed a section all of its own, because self-love is more than a step in the process: it is the foundation upon which all the other steps are built.

Once you begin to cultivate and practise self-love, your ability to manifest will become infinitely more powerful. Self-love empowers you to step into your light, to step into your greatness and to open up space for abundance to enter your life. Self-love tells the universe, 'I am worthy of love, I deserve success, I am ready to live my dreams,' and then, this is what you shall receive.

When we love ourselves, we embrace all that we truly are. When we love ourselves, we rise above fears, doubts, insecurities and limiting beliefs and we unlock our fullest potential.

There is no greater gift we can give ourselves than the gift of unconditional self-love.

Without self-love, you cannot manifest. There is no point in creating a vision board and talking about the life of your dreams if, day to day, you still treat yourself with disrespect.

So, how do you begin to cultivate self-love so that you can unlock your fullest manifesting power?

Well, first, I should clarify what self-love really means:

> Self-love means truly valuing your own wellbeing and happiness.
> Self-love means showing up for yourself and championing yourself.
> Self-love means letting go of judgement, regret and negative self-talk.
> Self-love means embracing the most authentic version of yourself.
> Self-love means offering yourself the same level of kindness, patience and forgiveness that you offer so freely to others.

There are a million ways we can practise self-love: we can make a conscious effort to practise and demonstrate more self-care, more self-respect, more self-discipline. We can create healthy boundaries, we can let go of things that no longer serve us, we can be mindful of the way in which we speak to ourselves. To practise self-love, we can fuel our minds, bodies and souls with nourishing food, thoughts and ideas. We can start saying no to the things we don't want to do. We can do more of the things that make us happy. We can practise meditation, we can journal, we can exercise, we can look after our skin, we can prioritize sleep, we can drink more water. We can offer ourselves more compassion and kindness. We can offer ourselves space to explore all the parts of us that make us unique. We can speak to ourselves in ways that are kind, encouraging and supportive. There are countless ways we can practise self-love – in fact, I could write an entire book on it.

But really, for me, cultivating self-love comes down to one thing: becoming aware of the choices we have and the decisions we make in each and every moment.

Every minute of every day we have an opportunity to practise and cultivate self-love. Every minute of every day we have to make a choice: do I choose to act in a way that is self-loving or in a way that is not? How you spend your time, what thoughts you choose to attach to, what perspective you choose to adopt, who you surround yourself with, what decisions you make, what behaviour you accept from others, how you govern yourself, what commitments you make, how you feed, fuel, nourish and move your body . . . *all of this matters.*

It *all* reflects your commitment to yourself, your wellbeing and your capacity for self-love. And it is that very commitment to yourself that shows the universe what you believe you are worthy of. **Remember: we manifest from our subconscious beliefs about what we deserve.**

BEGIN TO CULTIVATE SELF-LOVE

To start making decisions that will lead us to cultivate self-love, we must do three things.

1. Become aware and mindful

We can't make mindful choices if we aren't first aware of the choices available to us. We have to start taking time to pause and ask ourselves, 'Is there another way I could do this: a way that is more loving and more compassionate?' For example, if you've been trapped in the diet cycle for years and you find yourself cutting out food groups, skipping meals or obsessing over some new fad diet, then take a moment to consider whether this is really a compassionate and self-loving way to act, or whether there is another way you could choose to treat your body and approach your relationship with food? Could you stop skipping meals and attaching guilt to your food choices and work to replace those behaviour patterns with mindful and intuitive eating principles, for example? Or, if you watch the news first thing every morning and you find it always leaves you feeling frustrated, sad or anxious, ask yourself, 'Is this really helping me start my day in the best possible way? Could I make a more self-loving choice? Could I choose to start my day listening to music, journaling or incorporating a ten-minute yoga flow instead?'

2. Honour where you are

What we need day to day, moment to moment, is always going to change. Some days, we wake up and we feel ready to take on the world. Other days, we feel tired, flat and overwhelmed. Self-love means honouring yourself in each moment and making decisions that reflect how you are feeling at that time.

Get into the habit of checking in with yourself, and asking, 'Where am I at today? How do I feel and what do I need?' Imagine there is a scale of 1–10, 1 being at your lowest, and 10 being high-vibe superhero. What you need will differ depending on where you sit on that scale. If you're at a 3, let's say, then what you will need will likely be permission to rest, nourishing food and fresh air. But if you're at a 9, then you need to go ahead and use that energy to make choices that will propel you closer to your manifestation: get creative, be productive and move your body!

Don Miguel Ruiz wrote an incredible book called *The Four Agreements*. I recommend it to everyone, and one of the agreements is this: **Always do your best.** He writes, 'Your best is going to change from moment to moment, it will be different when you are healthy as opposed to sick, under any circumstance simply do your best and you will avoid self-judgment, self-abuse and regret.'

Self-love means giving yourself the space to be human, to acknowledge that we all feel differently day to day and to give yourself what you need, taking that into account.

3. Honour where you want to be tomorrow

Our lives are really just a culmination of the choices we make. When we act in ways that are self-loving, we honour not just what we need in the moment but also where we want to be tomorrow. So often, we make impulse decisions that satisfy us in the moment but negatively impact on our future selves. Anyone who has ever self-sabotaged (which I'll assume is every one of you reading this) will know what I mean. **But self-love is taking authority over that drive for instant satisfaction and instead making choices that will serve your future self.** For example, if you have a deadline for tomorrow and you choose instead to go out, or procrastinate by scrolling through Instagram, you are simply sabotaging what your future self needs. By making the choice to apply self-discipline and focus on meeting the deadline, however, you will have made a decision that honours what your future self needs and deserves: that is practising self-love.

> THE ULTIMATE PRACTICE OF SELF-LOVE IS PERFECTLY BALANCING WHAT YOU NEED TODAY WITH WHAT YOUR FUTURE SELF NEEDS TOMORROW.

Self-love manifests itself in every decision we make. Each and every day, commit to finding more ways to show up for yourself and demonstrate the compassion and love for yourself that you deserve. Keep doing this until it becomes the automatic way you govern your life. Keep practising until your cup is so full of self-love that it pours out to everything and everyone around you.

FORGIVENESS AND NON-JUDGEMENT

I couldn't talk about self-love without talking about forgiveness and non-judgement. How many times have you made a mistake or acted in ways you weren't proud of and then berated yourself for days, weeks or maybe years? When we hold on to shame, guilt, anger and resentment, we keep ourselves trapped in the past. We hold on to the energy of those experiences, which keeps our vibration low and holds us back from all that we want to manifest.

A client I began working with at the start of 2020 told me, 'I want to manifest it all': a new job, a new apartment, a feeling of true confidence and her soulmate. Within six months, everything she had wanted to manifest had come to her except for her soulmate. I started to ask her a little more about her past relationships and she revealed that she had been cheated on by her last two partners. She said that she had mostly 'blocked out the experience' but that, deep down, she still blamed herself for 'allowing' it to happen, and she constantly questioned whether she had somehow pushed them to cheat in the first place. She also said that she felt embarrassed that, as a successful career woman, she had not been able to see the signs right in front of her.

By attempting to block out the experience, she was not allowing herself to process all of her feelings surrounding it or to change the narrative of self-blame she had attached to the experience. Remember that trauma, pain and emotional distress are all energy; when they are not given the time and attention they need to be moved, released and healed, they live within our physical body. This means that when we try to 'block out' our past experiences, they have nowhere to go, so they stay within us, lowering our vibration and keeping us trapped in the past.

My client's experience was affecting her in another way, too: by blaming herself, she was creating a subconscious fear that history would inevitably repeat itself. It was only when we worked together to create a safe space to process the experience, to remove self-judgement and blame, to choose a new perspective and instead for her to offer herself complete compassion and non-judgement that she was able to remove her deeper, sub-conscious fears around meeting someone. I also encouraged her to work with one of my favourite mantras – 'My past does not dictate my future' – as a reminder that she has the power to change her future story. In doing the inner work, she was able to create room for her soulmate to enter her life. I received an email from her just recently and the subject line read, 'I met THE ONE!'

To unblock the path that leads us to our most magnificent future, we must let go of the parts of our past that cause us to feel those low-vibe emotions of shame, guilt or anger and instead offer ourselves complete non-judgement and forgiveness. To do this, we must acknowledge these three truths:

1. We were doing our best at the time.
2. There is always a valuable lesson to take from any and every experience.
3. We are not the same person we were then: we have since grown, evolved and matured.

▰▷ EXERCISE

I want you to think of something now that you are holding on to, something you are judging yourself for. Write down the experience you feel shame, guilt or anger around.

....
....
....
....

....
....
....
....

Now write a letter to your past self. Offer yourself compassion and kindness, and acknowledge and identify whether your actions were driven by pain or insecurity. You might write something such as 'I forgive you; you were doing your best, I know you were hurting at the time, it's OK, I love you.'

....
....
....
....
....
....
....
....

Now write down the lessons you learned from the experience and the value you have taken from it.

....
....
....
....
....
....
....
....

Repeat this exercise for anything you are still holding on to.

> **Note:** Every time I have done this exercise in a work-shop with others there has been a release of emotions and tears. If you find yourself crying or feeling particularly emotional while doing this, please allow space for that and allow yourself to feel liberated in doing so.

THE TRUTH IS THIS: BY LEARNING FROM YOUR MISTAKES AND EXPERIENCES AND BY EVOLVING THROUGH THEM YOU PRACTISE THE GREATEST FORM OF SELF-LOVE, WHICH IS TO GROW. *READ THAT AGAIN.*

Self-love is the driving force behind manifesting so we must cultivate it every day, through consistent practice and commitment. We must make choices to behave, to respond and to think in ways that build our self-worth and propel us into becoming our most powerful selves. We must offer ourselves non-judgement, compassion, forgiveness and kindness every day and in everything that we do. **No act of self-love is too great or too small. From drinking a glass of water to leaving a toxic relationship, everything we do defines who we are and who we become.**

> **Note:** I understand that, for some people, the idea of 'cultivating self-love' may seem incredibly daunting, especially if low self-worth and self-esteem currently seem to limit you at every turn. You may be thinking, 'Sure, it sounds easy in theory, but how do I suddenly just act like I love myself?' I understand your reservations; I was so

consumed by my self-loathing my entire life, I never thought it would be possible to reach a place where I could honestly say that I love who I am. When people said the word 'self-love', I would roll my eyes as though it was some imaginary concept that would never be within reach. But with time, practice and commitment I did reach it. And so can you.

Undoing years, or decades, of built-up insecurities, limiting beliefs and low self-esteem is not something that can be done overnight. But we can make the decision to begin making more loving choices right now. The decision to commit to self-love is half the battle. Then it is about choosing, each day and each moment, to cultivate more self-love in your life, little by little, because that is what you deserve. The more you do it, the easier it will become and the more natural it will feel.

While we cultivate self-love, we simultaneously work through the other steps in the manifesting process.

STEP 3

ALIGN YOUR BEHAVIOUR

ALIGNING YOUR BEHAVIOUR MEANS
SHOWING THE UNIVERSE, IN
ACTION, WHAT YOU BELIEVE YOU
DESERVE. THIS IS BECAUSE THE WAY
WE BEHAVE IS A DIRECT REFLECTION
OF OUR SELF-WORTH.

Aligning your behaviour means being *proactive* in your manifesting journey. Aligning your behaviour means **being the energy you want to attract**. Aligning your behaviour means stepping outside your comfort zone. Aligning your behaviour means aligning with your *most authentic self* because that self is the most magnetic version of you that exists.

This is the step that really differentiates the law of attraction from manifesting. The law of attraction says that what you think about most, you will attract into your life. But this can imply that there is a passiveness to the process. **Manifestation is not passive**: you cannot just be clear in your vision and then wait for it to appear.

> To step into your power and to really shift your energy to attract the abundance you deserve, you must start behaving in a way that is aligned with the most empowered version of yourself and not the version of you that has been *limited by fear and doubt*.

BE PROACTIVE IN YOUR MANIFESTATION

TO EFFECTIVELY MANIFEST, YOU MUST BE CLEAR IN YOUR VISION, KNOW THAT YOU ARE WORTHY OF IT AND THEN YOU MUST BE PROACTIVE IN MAKING IT HAPPEN.

For example, let's imagine you want to manifest a house in the countryside for you and your family. You must have a clear vision of the house, remove any fears or doubts surrounding it, trust that you are worthy of it *and then* you must be proactive in your search, for example by looking at property websites, speaking to estate agents or visiting the area to see if any houses are for sale. Similarly, if you wanted to manifest passing an exam, then you would need to be clear in your vision and then be proactive by committing time and energy to your revision and studies. No matter what you want to manifest, there will be an element of 'doing' that is needed. It is one of the biggest manifesting misconceptions that we can just visualize what we want and then expect it to show up for us without any effort required. I can certainly say that when manifesting my own career milestones, I did so only with the help of hard work, determination, persistence, self-discipline and motivation.

Being proactive requires fearlessness, a fearlessness that shows the universe 'I am worthy, I am deserving, and I am ready.'

Think about this: how many times have you intentionally avoided being proactive because the fear of failure overwhelmed you? I was speaking with a new client last month who told me about an idea she'd had to host a supper club. She wanted advice on how to find the courage to move forward with it. A little further along in the conversation, I discovered that she'd had the idea for nearly *two years*. During that time, she had absolutely everything in place to make it work, but her fear that 'no one would turn up' literally paralysed her from moving forward. This is not an unusual story. Almost every day I will hear a friend, family member or colleague tell me about a brilliant idea they have, an idea that they never follow through with because they don't believe they are good enough, worthy enough or capable enough to really make the idea come to life. How many times have *you* had an idea that you have let go because you were afraid you wouldn't be able to make it work? How many times have you been too afraid to reach out to someone out of fear of rejection? How many times have you allowed yourself to dismiss your dreams because they felt too far out of reach?

Procrastination and apprehension about taking action are so often driven by fear of failure: we avoid applying ourselves because it is easier not to try at all than to try and then fail. When this fear of failure is influencing us, it is easy to make a whole bunch of excuses about why we can't do something: we say we don't have the time, resources or energy. What do these excuses and lack of action say to the universe? They say, 'I'm not ready for it and I don't really believe I am worthy enough to receive it.' And as we know from Step 2: Remove Fear and Doubt (see page 23), this fear will block you from attracting the very thing that you desire.

BEING PROACTIVE TRANSCENDS THE FEAR OF FAILURE.

Imagine that you want to manifest a successful new business. Let me show you the difference between behaving in a way that is limited by fear and doubt (Version A) and behaving in a proactive way that is aligned with your vision and transcends fear and doubt (Version B).

Version A

Your fear of rejection prevents you from reaching out to new clients, your fear of judgement stops you from marketing yourself online, your doubts stop you from investing adequately into the business and your fear of failure blinds you from seeing potential opportunities and prevents you from taking risks.

You behave in a way that keeps you trapped in your comfort zone without potential for real growth and expansion.

Version B

You reach out to potential new clients, you promote yourself on every platform, you ask for advice from mentors, you are proactive in finding people to collaborate with, you see potential opportunities and grasp them, you find innovative ways to market yourself and you invest the time, energy and money needed for the business to succeed to the level that you desire.

It is clear to see how the way in which you behave would impact on your ability to manifest a successful new business. The person in version B will be proactively reaching their goals and, in doing so, will be much more effective in manifesting their dreams than the person in version A.

Another example of being proactive is this: if you want to manifest a loving relationship, you cannot simply put all the specific qualities and attributes of your perfect partner on a vision board and expect that person to appear. To manifest them into your life, you must align your behaviour accordingly. This would mean, first and foremost, **treating yourself with the level of respect and love you want to attract** (that is, by cultivating self-love). It would then mean being open to and proactive in creating opportunities to meet someone, whether that's joining a dating app, accepting offers to be set up by a friend or simply going to more social gatherings.

Whenever you want to manifest something into your life, you have to align your behaviour by taking action and being proactive. Aligning our behaviour shows the universe, 'I am ready, I am fearless, I am worthy.' And the universe will meet that fearlessness and readiness with abundance.

Some of you reading this may feel that the fears and doubts you identified in Step 2: Remove Fear and Doubt (see pages 33–5) are still very real. You may be asking, 'How can I align my behaviour when I don't feel like I've completed Step 2?' or 'How can I be proactive when I still feel afraid that I will fail?' The answer is that you work these steps in unison. Removing fear and doubt is an ongoing process, and it is something that you do *alongside* aligning your behaviour. Can you remember a time when you said you couldn't do something but decided to try anyway? Can you remember how proud of yourself you felt afterwards? Did that feeling of pride then enable you to continue to take steps forward?

I see this with my son, Wolfe, all the time. We went to a 'little gymnastics' class last week and there was a balancing beam he wanted to walk along. He was convinced he couldn't do it on his own, and he would reach for my hand to help him the whole way along. But when I gently let go and encouraged him to do it alone, I saw his face light up. He was so proud of himself. The next time he walked along the balancing beam, he looked at me as if to say, 'Don't worry, Mum, I've got this.' This is how you behave in a way that transcends your fears and doubts: you do something, despite feeling afraid, and in taking action you build your self-belief and self-worth, which in turn drives your manifesting power and helps you to continue to take action going forward. It's an upward cycle. Essentially, you just need to **feel the fear and do it anyway.**

You know that saying 'Fake it until you make it'? Well, I heard a better version recently that made much more sense to me and fits perfectly with this step:

FAKE IT UNTIL YOU BECOME IT.

Sometimes we just have to take a leap of faith and trust that by acting in ways that align with the idea of who we want to be, we will take ourselves closer to becoming it. Remember, back in Step 1: Be Clear in Your Vision (see page 14), I said that one of the most important questions you can ask yourself on your manifesting journey is 'Who do I want to become?' When we have clarity on this person, on the most empowered version of ourselves, we can begin to behave in ways that align us with them from this moment.

To give you an example, I have a friend who for many years wanted to work as a life coach to help other men on their healing journeys. He had completed a coaching course and spent most of his spare time helping the people around him, but he held a great deal of fear around turning this into a profession. He didn't trust that his experience and understanding had enough value to deserve payment, so he avoided letting anyone know that he was a certified coach and never risked exposing himself to failure. After I'd spent some time working through this with him and introducing him to the world of manifesting, he decided to start 'faking it until he became it'. I said to him, 'If you were already a successful coach, what would you be doing with your time? How would you be marketing yourself and what action would you take?' He gave me a list of things that he could think of, then I told him to go ahead and do them. Within days, he had set up an Instagram page as a men's coach, connected with other men in the industry, begun creating self-development content, advertised his own one-on-one sessions, and kept himself open to any and every opportunity that presented itself. Over the course of twelve months, slowly but surely he built up his presence in the wellness industry, created a loyal and engaged community of followers, was working with clients every single week and had hosted a free webinar for men in which he had put together a panel of eight influential men's mental health experts. By aligning his behaviour with who he wanted to be, even when he was unsure of it himself, the universe rewarded him.

Sometimes, we just have to fake it until we become it.

> **Note:** For anyone suffering from imposter syndrome, 'fake it till you become it' can be a great phrase to return to. When we start a new career or throw ourselves into something unknown, we can experience self-doubt that tells us we aren't qualified, skilled or knowledgeable enough to do what we are doing. This is totally normal, and there aren't many people who *haven't* felt this way! Remind yourself that by aligning your behaviour, you can step into the most empowered version of yourself from now. With time, you will start to accept and believe the truth: that you are deserving of the position, that you are enough and that you are worthy of thriving.

Here is an exercise that can help you identify some of the ways you can align your behaviour with your manifestation by being proactive and taking action.

✏️ EXERCISE: BEHAVE THE WAY YOUR FUTURE SELF WOULD

I want you to take a moment now to imagine your future self. I want you to really sink into this exercise and fill your visualization with details. Imagine the version of you that is at the height of your manifesting powers and has drawn in all that you could want in your life.

Make it feel as real as possible, bringing your most magnificent self to life.

Now ask yourself the following questions:

How do I behave?
What do I do to live in such a self-loving, empowered and magnetic way?

List five things that your future self does, informed by the most powerful version of yourself.

1. . . . .
. . . .
2. . . . .
. . . .
3. . . . .
. . . .
4. . . . .
. . . .
5. . . . .
. . . .

These are the things I want you to start doing in your life right now to take you even closer to meeting your future self.

Whenever you think about the person you want to become, think of ways in which you can align your behaviour with that version of yourself from this very moment. Show the universe, in action, that you are ready to embody them, because *they already exist within you*.

GETTING COMFORTABLE WITH DISCOMFORT

As you begin aligning your behaviour with your manifestation and your future self, it is important to recognize that it won't all feel easy and it certainly won't always feel comfortable. In fact, aligning your behaviour will *require* you to step into a place of discomfort. Let me explain why.

Our subconscious finds comfort in what is familiar to us, even if what is familiar is not necessarily what is good for us. This is because familiarity feels safe. When we act in new ways, we will be encountering things that are unfamiliar. This unfamiliarity will feel uncomfortable and therefore unsafe. It will feel so uncomfortable that our subconscious will desperately try to pull us back into what it's used to so that it can feel safe again. This is why we self-sabotage.

We do what feels
comfortable

Our subconscious
craves familiarity

We decide to
make a change

We question the
changes made

The cycle of
SELF-SABOTAGE

We take the steps
to change

We feel
uncomfortable

We start to
feel good

This feels different

For example, let's imagine that you are someone who has always taken a back seat or shied away from the spotlight. You've essentially cast yourself in a supporting role in the story of your life. After years of living like this, that is simply where your subconscious will feel most comfortable: when you hide in the shadow of others. So, when you decide to make a change and say, 'Now is the time to step into my light, to show the world what I have to offer and finally be the protagonist of my own story,' your subconscious will panic and try to pull you back into comfortable territory by encouraging you, on a subconscious level, to self-sabotage. It might do this by sabotaging opportunities for you to speak out or be seen or heard, or by subconsciously encouraging you to surround yourself with people who bring you down or whose energy will overshadow yours.

I had a friend who was trying to become more confident when meeting new people. She signed up to a parent-baby group that she began going to every week and being able to meet and connect with other new mums was really helping her to build her self-esteem. She seemed to be making an internal shift, but then, a couple of months later, I realized that she hadn't gone back to the meet-up in weeks; every time she arranged to go, something would 'coincidentally' come up, for example she would have double-booked, she would suddenly feel too tired, or she would find herself unexpectedly busy on the day. I told her that all of this was subconscious self-sabotage at play, and only when she could recognize that could she begin to move past it.

Another example might be that your goal is to feel healthy, energized and physically fit. Your vision is clear and you see yourself waking up with energy and vitality and feeling fit enough to play outside with your children for hours on end. To reach this goal, you will first have to be proactive in changing your behaviour. For example, instead of making excuses not to exercise or to over-indulge in food which make you feel sluggish, you will have to commit to an exercise routine or to making healthier, more nourishing food choices. In other words, **you have to be proactive by taking action**. After doing this for some time, you will begin to see and feel a difference: your confidence will begin to grow. This is when your subconscious will panic. It doesn't care that you are feeling good, it just cares that you feel different, and different, for your subconscious, doesn't feel safe. So it will encourage you to self-sabotage by convincing you to binge, to skip your workouts or to give up on your goals altogether. Sound familiar?

I certainly used to find myself trapped in self-sabotaging cycles all the time. I was so comfortable in feeling sad, alone and full of self-loathing that every time I committed to making changes and started to feel better I would self-sabotage with food, alcohol, drugs, cigarettes and toxic relationships. It was only when I became aware of what my subconscious was trying to do that I was able to overcome the urges to self-sabotage and instead stay focused on where I wanted to be. I could then sit through the discomfort until I established a new familiarity – and that is how you create real and lasting change.

Whenever we enter a period of transformation and we begin to align our behaviour with what we want to attract into our lives, we must simultaneously expect a period of discomfort and then make a **conscious commitment** to accept it and sit through it. We must resist the urge to self-sabotage, and we **must learn to live in this new, empowered place until it feels like home**. Because, when we live in a place that is not limited by our fears and doubts, we unlock all the abundance of the universe.

STEPPING OUT OF YOUR COMFORT ZONE

Once we have understood the self-sabotaging cycle and the requirement to be OK with some degree of discomfort, we can align our behaviour in the most powerful and magnetic way of all: by regularly, and continuously, stepping outside our comfort zone.

> TO MANIFEST CHANGE, WE MUST FIRST CREATE CHANGE. WE MUST DO SOMETHING DIFFERENT, WE MUST CHALLENGE OUR FEARS AND DOUBTS, WE MUST ACT AS OUR FUTURE SELF WOULD ACT AND WE MUST SHOW THE UNIVERSE HOW READY AND WILLING WE ARE TO STEP INTO OUR POWER.

On any manifesting journey, you will be required to step outside your comfort zone. It is non-negotiable. Every single time you step outside your comfort zone, you attract abundance to you. This is because magic happens outside your comfort zone.

People often say to me, 'I'm thinking of quitting my job. Should I do it?' or 'I've had this idea for a new venture. Should I go for it?' My answer is always the same: *absolutely, yes*. When you begin to realize that you have the power within you to create a wonderful, exciting and abundant life for yourself, you will naturally start to think of ways that you can step outside your comfort zone. **The journey of manifesting is always accompanied with inspiration, creativity and an influx of ideas that will just come to you, seemingly out of nowhere.** You might be meditating, about to fall asleep, out for a walk or talking to a friend, and an idea will flow in. I like to think of these ideas as little gifts from the universe. They come to you for a reason: they are an opportunity for you to step outside your comfort zone so that you can create the change you need to get to where you want to be. They are an opportunity for you to show the universe that you are not held back by fear and doubt. When the ideas come, do not ignore them. Instead, make the self-loving decision to take action and step outside your comfort zone.

Here are a few ways to help you step outside your comfort zone and into your manifesting power:

1. Be clear on your why

Before stepping outside your comfort zone, be clear on *why* you want to do so. The 'why' is what will drive you through the discomfort. The 'why' is what will keep you focused and connected to your vision and keep you motivated if you are met with any challenges or obstacles.

FAQ:

Q: How do I find out what my 'why' is?

A: Whenever you think of something you want to manifest, ask yourself, 'What do I think achieving that goal will do for me energetically, emotionally, physically, mentally or spiritually? How will it affect my day-to-day life and my feelings of peace, contentment, self-love and joy?'

For example, let's imagine that your friend tells you that a position is opening up at the firm she works at and the role feels just perfect for you. You immediately decide to apply but then see that, as part of the application process, you have to film yourself talking to camera. If you are someone who has always struggled with being in front of the camera, this would require you to sit through some discomfort while you step outside your comfort zone. So, you would really need to identify your 'why' so that it can drive you through the discomfort. It could be 'This job would enable me to work in an area I am truly passionate about. I would feel excited to go to work in the morning and doing something I actually love would make me feel more at peace, it would bring more joy into my life and it would improve the overall quality of my life.' By remaining focused on your 'why', you will be able to gain the momentum and courage required to film the clip, *despite* feeling a little uncomfortable or afraid, because you can clearly see the bigger picture and the end goal.

2. Remove excuses

Excuses are nothing more than a form of self-sabotage. They give us an 'out'. Excuses come in many forms but, most commonly, they sound like this: 'I'm too busy'; 'I'm too tired'; 'It's too difficult'; 'I'm not ready'; 'I'll do it another day'; 'I don't have the resources'; 'It didn't work last time I tried'; 'I won't be able to do it perfectly'; 'I'm not good enough.'

But **we must expose our excuses for what they really are: an expression of our fear and doubt**. They come out to hold us back from moving forward and stepping into our power when we subconsciously feel that we are not yet ready for greatness. The way to remove excuses is to question every aspect of them. By questioning them, we take away their power.

The next time you say to yourself, 'I am too busy,' ask yourself, 'Why am I telling myself that? What am I afraid of? What would happen if I removed the excuse?'

3. Don't give up when faced with challenges

When we step outside our comfort zone, everything will be new, which means that inevitably we will be faced with some obstacles to overcome.

> ONE OF THE MOST COMMON CHARACTERISTICS OF ANY SUCCESSFUL INDIVIDUAL IS THEIR ABILITY AND WILLINGNESS TO PERSIST THROUGH CHALLENGES.

I'm sure that every one of us can remember a time when we have buckled and given up at the first hurdle. Why do we do this? Because challenges trigger our insecurities and test our self-worth. If we are faced with something that we find difficult, we question our own abilities, or if a plan falls through, we worry that we are simply 'unlucky'. We allow challenges to reinforce our limiting and subconscious beliefs that we are not worthy of having the things we desire most. So, then what do we do? We run — we run because our innate tendency is to escape from things that make us feel 'bad'. But if you want to manifest successfully, you must resist the urge to give up and instead find an alternative way to move forward.

I have always been obsessed with reading, watching and hearing the stories of incredibly successful people, from CEOs to world-famous musicians. What I find most inspiring about their journeys is learning about the times they had to persist in the face of challenge, or when they had to think of creative new ways to overcome a potential deterrent to their dreams. It reminds me that the road to success, or to manifesting everything you want, is not always easy or straightforward. You have to show up for yourself, take action, and keep going, even when you might feel like throwing in the towel. I know that if I had given up at every challenge or opportunity that came my way, I would never, ever have succeeded in manifesting all the things that I have into my life. My own story was not a case of visualizing what I wanted, taking action and then seeing all of it come to me straight away. I still had to face rejections and hurdles. But I never allowed them to stop me from moving forward. I never let them derail me or distract me from my goal. In fact, I flat out refuse to be defeated by obstacles. When something doesn't go right first time, I simply think of another way to do it.

Challenges are an inevitable part of life and, rather than seeing them as limitations, I urge you to begin to see them as gifts and opportunities. Challenges give us the chance to show up for ourselves, to learn something new, to build strength, knowledge and resilience. Challenges push us in new directions and give us new perspectives. Make a choice, right now, to be guided by challenges that you may face instead of being put off by them. In doing so, you send a message to the universe that says, '**I am stronger than the challenge I am faced with,**' and then the universe will reward your self-belief with abundance.

4. The 5-second rule

One of my favourite speakers, Mel Robbins, has an amazing exercise that you can use whenever you are faced with an opportunity to step out of your comfort zone but are feeling fear or trepidation about doing so. She calls it 'the 5-second rule'. Mel says, 'The moment your instincts fire up, but you feel yourself hesitate, that's when you use the "5-Second Rule".' You have five seconds. Start counting backwards to yourself from five to one, then move before you reach zero. She says that, 'If you have an impulse to act on a goal, you must physically move within 5 seconds or your brain will kill the idea.'

I used this technique myself before I hosted my first ever in-person workshop. I was about to go on stage for the first time and my nerves had got the better of me. I was backstage behind a curtain, the microphone was on, I could hear people settling down, ready for me to begin, and then imposter syndrome hit me. What the hell was I doing, hosting a self-love workshop? I'm not a public speaker, I'm not experienced enough, I'm going to let them all down. This was a stupid idea. My inner critic was trying to paralyse me from stepping on to my stage. I counted down, '5 . . . 4 . . . 3 . . .' and then, *bam*, I moved, I put one foot in front of the other, smiled at all the faces in front of me and began to talk. Within ten minutes, I knew something for sure: this was exactly where I was supposed to be. I suddenly felt so at home as I spoke to all these wonderful men and women in front of me about the power and importance of self-love. Now, countless workshops later, I use that technique before I step on to any stage.

I'LL SAY THIS AGAIN:
MAGIC HAPPENS OUTSIDE
YOUR COMFORT ZONE.

CREATE HEALTHY HABITS

By now, I hope it is clear that our self-worth is integral to our ability to manifest and that the way in which we behave acts as an indicator to the universe as to how high or low our self-worth is.

One way that we can align our behaviour to raise our self-worth and boost our manifesting powers is to deliberately incorporate high-vibe daily practices into our routines. We can take self-love practices and turn them into heathy habits.

SOME OF MY FAVOURITE SELF-LOVE PRACTICES

Journaling, mantras, affirmations, meditation, daily walks, skincare routines, long baths, self-care, breathwork, exercise, yoga, gratitude.

Developing healthy habits is an effective way to align our behaviour so that we can manifest more effortlessly. For me, healthy habits are the basis of any self-development journey. Our habits become our foundation, and when we change our habits, we change our life. **True and lasting change is really created in the small changes that you make day to day.** So, to use habits to drive us towards the things we want to manifest into our lives, we must start forming habits that are in line with our future self.

HEALTHY HABITS HELP US TO
EMBODY THE PERSON THAT WE
WANT TO BECOME; IN OTHER
WORDS, BE THE ENERGY WE WANT
TO ATTRACT.

For example, if you want to manifest becoming a successful leader in business, you can begin to form the habits a leader in business might have, such as waking up early, making daily to-do lists, having a daily meditation practice to help manage stress or overwhelm, or carving out daily dedicated learning time. In committing to these practices from now, you begin to align your behaviour with the person you want to become. Your habits help you to raise your vibration to match the energy of your future self.

Our habits and our daily practices change our lives.

Let's look at how different your day might look if you were someone that did not incorporate daily practices in the morning (Person A), as opposed to someone that did (Person B).

Person A
You wake up to your alarm, roll over and immediately begin scrolling through your social media feed. After ten minutes you get up, turn on the news, jump in the shower and quickly get ready before rushing through your breakfast and heading to work.

Person B
You wake up early to give yourself time to enjoy your daily practices, you roll over and press play on a ten-minute positive affirmations track before getting out of bed. Then you mindfully enjoy your morning coffee ritual before exercising for twenty minutes, shower and get dressed while listening to your favourite music, then sit down to eat a nutritious and delicious breakfast before heading to work.

Person B has done nothing extraordinary here: they have simply added three or four simple self-loving practices into their routine and committed to making the time for them. Yet can you imagine how differently the rest of their day might look compared to person A's? Can you imagine, then, how different person B's entire week, month or year would look compared to person A's?

Motivational author John C. Maxwell says, '**You will never change your life until you change something you do daily. The secret of your success is found in your daily routine.**'

✏️ EXERCISE

In the box below, write down three daily practices you will begin to incorporate into your life.

Make a commitment to yourself to do them every day for sixty-six days (the number of days it is said to take to form a habit).

For example:
1. I will wake up at 7 a.m. every day.
2. I will journal every evening before bed instead of scrolling through my phone.
3. I will exercise every morning, whether that's a walk, a stretch or a HIIT class.

1. ....
....
2. ....
....
3. ....
....

Continue to incorporate more and more healthy habits when you feel you are able to (don't overwhelm yourself with too many at once). The more healthy habits we have in a day, the more opportunities we have to practise self-love and increase our ability to manifest all the things we want.

AUTHENTICITY

'I had no idea that being your authentic self could make me as rich as I've become. If I had, I'd have done it a lot earlier.'

OPRAH WINFREY

As well as incorporating daily practices into your routine, being proactive in reaching your goals, becoming the energy you want to attract and stepping outside your comfort zone, aligning your behaviour also requires you to live authentically. It requires you to align what you do with what you think and who you really want to be.

Authenticity is an essential ingredient for successful manifestation because we become our most magnetic when we live and express our truth. Just think about the most magnetic people you know, the ones who walk into a room and light it up, the people who seem to always have others gravitating towards them. They are, most often, the people who are just completely, unapologetically and authentically themselves. They are proud of who they are, comfortable in their own skin and are never afraid to be different or to stand out.

I find, time and time again, that when anyone makes the decision to stop pretending to be something they are not and to instead embrace their most authentic selves, they *thrive*. I have received testimonials from countless men and women who have attended one of my workshops and then used the motivation from the session to let go of jobs, people and ideas that were not in line with their truth. They always describe the same story: once they let go of them, they created space to nurture the things that supported their most authentic selves. For example, starting a new job doing something they were actually passionate about, finally speaking out about things that mattered to them or only surrounding themselves with people who they felt truly understood by. Without exception, as soon as they began to do these things, they flourished. **We are unstoppably magnetic when we are unapologetically ourselves**.

So, how do we become connected with our most authentic selves? We must first learn to **let go** of who we think we should be, who other people expect us to be and who we once were. Only then can we uncover who we really are now.

From our earliest years, we search for clues from the people around us to tell us how to behave and how to be loved. We take note of when we do something that makes us lovable, and we do more of it. As we grow up, we continue this pattern: moulding ourselves based on the feedback we get from our family, friends and community. We are taught to look for external validation and associate our sense of self-worth with the opinions and judgement of others. It is through this process that we develop our 'people-pleasing' tendencies, which become the enemy of authenticity.

To begin the journey of discovering our most authentic selves, we must first gain awareness: every time we take action, we must recognize that we have a choice to make. The choice is this: 'Do I behave to please others or do I behave to honour myself?' If we choose the former, we inevitably sacrifice aligning our behaviour towards our own goals, dreams or visions.

ENERGY IS DIRECTIONAL: IT IS
SIMPLY IMPOSSIBLE TO DIRECT OUR
ENERGY TOWARDS SEEKING
EXTERNAL VALIDATION WHILE
SIMULTANEOUSLY DIRECTING IT
TOWARDS THE PERSON THAT WE
WANT TO BE OR THE THING THAT
WE WANT TO MANIFEST.

I often speak to Wade, the father of my son, about authenticity, as he is incredibly passionate about helping others discover their truth and express their most authentic selves. Wade uses the metaphor of a garden to explain this process. He says:

'Imagine yourself as a garden. Your deepest sense of self-love, worth and truth are the soil from which everything grows. Your conditioning and your life experiences so far mean that the garden is filled with different plants, but not all of them have been put there by you. Some of them are weeds which keep you from growing, others are plants that are not native to who you really are and some simply no longer feel like they belong in your garden. The process of expressing your most authentic self begins first by identifying those weeds and unwanted plants and very gently removing them. Getting down to the roots and taking them out so that the soil of your garden can be free of anything harmful. Then, once you feel like you have cleared the garden of those weeds and plants that are no longer necessary, of all your limiting beliefs and those ideas that do not serve you, you can begin to choose what goes in. You can nourish and care for the plants that empower you and you can choose new ones that express who you really are and who you want to be. You get to choose exactly what your garden looks like. You get to create every part of it and then nurture it with gentleness, compassion, love and respect. Ultimately, you deserve be a person of your own making: one who powerfully and beautifully celebrates who you choose to be, regardless of anyone else's ideas or opinions.'

The journey to discover and express your most authentic self is one that will take time, but one that will be worth every step. The more you are connected to who you really are and what you really desire, the more magnetic you become and the greater your manifesting power. Every time you act, ask yourself, 'Is this aligned with what I think, what I believe and who I want to be?'

Aligning your behaviour is manifesting in action. The things you do day to day, the way you behave, the way you act and the way you treat yourself: it *all* matters. The universe is responding to everything that you do.

Aligning your behaviour requires you to be proactive, take action, embody the person you want to become, move beyond your limiting beliefs or fears, step outside of your comfort zone, live authentically and cultivate self-love through daily practice, creating healthy habits and committing to your own wellbeing.

STEP 4

OVERCOME TESTS FROM THE UNIVERSE

On any manifesting journey, you will be presented with tests from the universe that you must overcome before you can progress any further. They come into your life to test your self-worth and your trust in the manifesting process. Tests can come in the forms of obstacles, people or challenges, or as something that asks you to settle for less than you deserve.

This step is an extension of Step 3: Align Your Behaviour (see page 61). In overcoming tests from the universe, you align your behaviour with high self-worth and learn to trust in the power of manifesting.

The easiest way for me to explain what a test from the universe looks like is to give you some examples.

Let's imagine that you want to manifest your perfect partner. Before you meet 'the one', you will likely be presented with a test from the universe to overcome first. The test is there to see how worthy you *really* believe you are of attracting them into your life.

In this scenario, the test may come in the form of 'the ex'. The reappearance of an ex is often accompanied with that enticing feeling of familiarity. They present you with an easy opportunity to head back towards something that feels comfortable, even though it isn't right for you. The choice here is this: do you invest your time and energy into something that you already know doesn't work or do you stay committed to your future and make a choice to physically and (more importantly) energetically walk away from your past and close the door firmly behind you?

The test of the ex is so common that I often tell people that if a previous partner suddenly reappears in their life, they can be sure that their soulmate is close behind (if the test is passed, of course). There is something incredibly liberating and empowering about being able to say to yourself, 'I am officially closing the door to my past.' But to do this properly, you must do it *fully*. I have heard so many men and women tell me they are not invested in the idea of getting back with their ex but then continue to message them or see them 'casually'. They are leaving the door open. They do it because it provides them with comfort, connection, attention, validation and distraction, but engaging with something that isn't right for you, no matter how casual you think it is, will block your path to your manifestation. This is because engaging with it says to the universe, 'I don't trust that what I really want is coming,' or 'I need to find my self-worth in someone else,' in which case you will continue to attract what matches both that doubt and low self-worth.

Finding closure within yourself on an energetic level is the most powerful and effective way to clear space for what is meant to enter your life. Whenever you see an opportunity to step away from someone or something that is no longer serving you, take it. You *must* clear the path so that you can meet your future self with ease.

Here is another example of a test that might appear when you are working towards manifesting your perfect partner. You go on a few dates with someone new and there is immediate chemistry between you both. They seem to tick a lot of your 'boxes', making you feel hopeful that they're the one you've been wanting to manifest. But within a few days or weeks, you start to sense something is off; they are blowing hot and cold or they are not showing you the respect that you deserve. This is a *clear* test. The universe is asking you something: how much do you really value yourself? How worthy of *true love* do you really think you are? Are you going to settle for someone who doesn't seem willing to commit to you?

If you choose to settle for that person and ignore the red flags that are right in front of you, you will block your manifestation. The reason for this is because in choosing to ignore the warning signs you send this message to the universe: 'I am afraid I won't meet anyone else, and I don't believe that I will find anyone who can truly love me and commit to me the way I deserve.' **Remember: to manifest what you want, you must believe you are worthy of it and your behaviour must align with that belief.** So, if you choose to walk away from this person, you show the universe, in action, that you know you are worthy of a deeper, stronger connection. The universe will respond by bringing your soulmate to you.

Any time that you make a choice to 'settle' in any area of your life, you will block yourself from manifesting all of the things you desire most. This is because the act of settling for less than you deserve is driven from that low-vibe place of fear and doubt: fear that you aren't really worthy of having what you truly desire and doubt that you will ever be able to manifest your dreams.

If you want to become an effortless manifestor, then mastering this is key. Begin to look at all the areas of your life and ask yourself, 'Where am I settling for something less than ideal? Where am I compromising my self-worth?' For example, do you currently have toxic friendships in your life that you can't seem to let go of? Almost every client I've ever worked with has had a toxic person in their life who constantly drains them, negatively affects their confidence and lowers their vibe. They stay in the friendship because they are either scared to offend or upset the other person by walking away, or they worry that, without them, they will feel more alone. Toxic friendships and relationships are another example of a test, and only when we find the courage and inner strength to step away from them will we open up space for healthier relationships to enter our lives. **Remember: your time and energy are your most valuable assets, so use them wisely.**

FAQ:

Q: What if I fail a test?

A: I often get people messaging me saying, 'Roxie, I think I've ruined it. I went back to my ex and we were together for a month and then he cheated on me again. I feel like such an idiot. Have I ruined everything?' The answer is *no*, of course not. Remember: the universe is on your side. It's just waiting for you to see the light. It doesn't punish you if you don't get it right first time. Whenever you make the energetic shift to overcome your test, you will be rewarded with abundance.

Tests don't just come in the form of people. The tests that you really need to look out for are the ones that appear to be exactly what you were waiting for but, when you look a little closer, you realize something just isn't quite right. For example, if you are on the hunt for your perfect house and you come across one that is 'almost' it, but not quite, do you take it, out of fear of not finding something better? Or do you walk away and wait for the right one?

A close friend of mine, a make-up artist, wanted to manifest being signed by a particular agency that represents some of the most well-respected creatives in the world. He wrote down the agency's name on his vision board and began working on cultivating self-love, removing some of his limiting beliefs and aligning his behaviour by uploading regular content on his social media channels to showcase his work and accepting as much client work as he could to build his portfolio and experience. A couple of months passed and he was feeling much more confident in himself and had developed his own authentic niche within his field. Then he got an email: an agency wanted to sign him, but it was not the agency of his dreams. He had an important choice to make: should he say yes out of fear that he wouldn't be able to manifest signing with his dream agency? Or should he turn them down, knowing it was not really what he wanted, and wait? It was a hard decision to make. These decisions often are; they require you to demonstrate unwavering confidence and it can feel unnerving to turn down something that is a 'good offer' just because it isn't exactly what you were after. My friend said that in not taking the offer to go with that agency, he felt he was being ungrateful, or even greedy. I reminded him that knowing what you want and holding out for it is neither of those things. After a few days of considered thought, he made the empowered decision to turn down the offer. Five months later, he signed with the agency he'd put on his vision board.

At any given time, we can choose to adopt a *scarcity mindset* or an *abundance mindset*. A scarcity mindset says that there is not enough love, happiness or success to go around for everyone. It comes from a place of lack. An abundance mindset trusts that there is plenty enough for everyone. At every stage of the manifesting process, adopting an abundance mindset is integral, and it is particularly important when overcoming tests from the universe. Whenever a test appears, you can choose to respond from a scarcity mindset (there is not enough to go around) or an abundance mindset (there is more than enough for everyone and there is an abundance of opportunity). Imagine you are in search of your perfect pair of jeans. You walk into a shop and see a gorgeous-looking pair on a hanger in front of you. You optimistically head to the changing rooms to try them on. When you do, you realize they aren't quite right for you. At that point, because you know that that there is an abundance of differently styled jeans in the world, you would quite happily put those ones back on the hanger and continue your search for the perfect pair. You wouldn't waste time thinking, 'There is only a handful of jeans in the world so I'd better take these in case I don't find something better.' You have to apply this abundance mindset to *everything* in your life to be able to manifest the things you truly desire. Put back the things that aren't right for you and know that you are worthy, and deserving, of having the things that are.

As well as being stuck in a scarcity mindset, one of the reasons we often fail tests from the universe is because our impatience gets the better of us. When we want something we can sometimes ignore the details of our vision and go for the next-best thing, if that means we get to have it more quickly. For example, have you ever redecorated your house or your office? If so, you'll know that lead times for buying key pieces of furniture can be months because they are often made to order, especially if you are looking for something particularly unique or special. So, in the process of refurnishing your space, you are always met with a choice: do you find something else that isn't quite perfect but will arrive sooner or do you wait patiently so that you can create the perfect interior space that matches the vision you originally had in mind? Manifesting your best life is a little like refurnishing your home. Sometimes you have to wait just a little longer than you hoped so that you can create the perfect space to live in. The space that you've always dreamed of, the space you first created on your vision board.

WHEN THINGS DON'T GO YOUR WAY

Other types of tests we are presented with are challenges we face when things either don't go as we had planned or we face rejection. It could be a trip you've been looking forward to being cancelled, an offer on a flat or a house falling through, an unexpected bill coming through the post, not getting into the university you applied to or learning that a potential love interest has met someone else. All these situations have the potential to derail you and quickly rock your confidence and your trust in the manifesting process. But here is what you need to know: **when things don't go the way you hoped they would, you are in fact being given your greatest opportunity to show up for yourself while building inner strength, resilience and courage.**

Imagine that you are an actor wanting to manifest a lead role in a TV series. Your manifesting journey might look something like this: on your vision board, you write down the genre of show you want to appear in, the channel you want to be on, the salary you would like to receive per episode, perhaps even the name of the director of the show. You then work on identifying and removing fear and doubt and you align your behaviour by investing in acting lessons, committing time and energy to your auditions and being proactive in spending time with other people in the industry from whom you can learn. Then your agent calls you with the 'perfect role'. You think, 'Oh my goodness, this is *it*!' You give the audition everything you've got, wait patiently and then they call you to say that you didn't land the job. You inevitably feel crushed. After you have processed your disappointment you have a choice: do you allow this to strip you of all your confidence and undo all the hard work you've put in, or do you accept that it simply wasn't the right fit for you, stay in your power and move forward? To put it simply, do you choose to lose faith or do you choose to trust that there is something better out there for you?

When I first decided to launch my own podcast series, 'The Moments that Made Me', in which I ask each of my guests to take me through three of the defining moments that shaped their lives, I had to first reach out to people to see if they would like to be guests. This was something that terrified me from the outset: would people think I was annoying for asking them? Would anyone say yes? Would the podcast be a total failure? I had always been so scared to ask people for favours, out of a fear of being judged or rejected. But the podcast was important to me so I knew I had to step out my comfort zone and just go for it. So, I got out a pen and paper and wrote a list of all the people I had connections to and could reach out to. The first person I messaged was a very well-known celebrity who was a judge on a reality show at the time. I texted them nervously and asked if they would like to be a guest. I got a reply straight away. I opened it and it said something along the lines of them being sorry, but that they wouldn't feel comfortable sharing their personal life and so wouldn't be able to help me on this project, but wished me good luck! I remember feeling sick to my stomach – I immediately felt so embarrassed that I had asked them and I took their response as complete rejection. Then I remembered that I had a choice. I could choose to let it derail me and my confidence and stop the journey before it even began or I could choose to acknowledge that this was simply a test from the universe for me to overcome. I reframed my thinking: this person's decision not to share their story was not a personal rejection, it was a completely valid and understandable reason, and it did not mean that everyone I asked would have the same response. In that moment, I sent out messages to five more people. They all said yes. By the end of 2020, I had recorded twenty-eight episodes, the *exact* number of episodes I had put on my vision board at the start of the year (I honestly couldn't even tell you why I chose this figure; I just did!). And then, in May 2021 the billboard for my podcast was put on ninety advertising boards all around London! Seeing my podcast advertised around the city was so incredibly special, and I was bursting with pride. If I hadn't stepped out of my comfort zone and then overcome the test put in front of me, it would never have been possible.

The Russian philosopher Helena Blavatsky is thought to have been one of the first people to write about manifesting, back in the late nineteenth century. In *The Secret Doctrine*, she wrote, 'Do not be afraid of your difficulties. Do not wish you could be in other circumstances than you are. For when you have made the best of adversity, it becomes the stepping stone to a splendid opportunity.' When I first read this, I could not stop smiling. This beautiful passage, which was written over a hundred years ago, supported something that I had intuitively known to be true: that when we overcome tests from the universe, we are rewarded with new opportunity.

> WHEN WE OVERCOME TESTS, WE BUILD SOMETHING WITHIN US: AN INNER STRENGTH THAT IS MAGNETIC.

I received a message on Instagram from someone who had attended one of my manifesting webinars that said, 'I have been working on my manifesting process for the last few weeks and then I got a job interview at my dream company last Monday. I'm new to the industry and I couldn't believe I had even been asked. I really thought I'd manifested what I wanted, but then I didn't get the job. I feel so lost and broken and I don't know what to do.' I felt for her. That feeling of disappointment after days or weeks of experiencing hopeful excitement can feel so painful. But again, there was a choice to make. She could choose to give up, to wallow in the low-vibe feeling of rejection, or she could choose to reframe her internal response. She could instead choose to say, 'Wasn't it incredible that, as someone new to the industry, I was able to manifest an interview for a dream role so quickly? I can take real value from what I learned in the interview preparation, and in the interview itself, and that will benefit me when I find the perfect role for me.' This is a high-vibe, empowered response to rejection. I offered her a new perspective and explained that this was all part of the process. I encouraged her to recognize the test, reframe her thinking and keep her vibe high by listening to some career affirmations every night before bed. She messaged me three weeks later, saying, 'I just wanted to say thank you so much for helping me to reframe things when I messaged you before. I've actually managed to achieve all that I've wanted since your last manifesting workshop. Despite the initial doubt and frustration, plus not seeing the rewards as quickly as I would have liked to, what I've learned has paid dividends. I'm on my way to my new job for an induction and I start tomorrow.'

Sometimes, the universe knows you are worth more than the thing you desire. It doesn't give you the things that you want because it wants to give you something better. Trust that the universe is always looking out for your best interests. If the person you've been seeing ghosts you four months into your relationship, then accept that they were not the one for you. If a plan is cancelled at the last minute, it wasn't meant to be. Manifesting is sometimes just about dusting yourself off, standing tall and taking whatever value you can from the experience, knowing that there is always a lesson to be learned and something greater on the other side.

I use the word 'choose' a lot in this book, and that's because our power to choose is one of our greatest manifesting tools. We can choose what visions we create, what thoughts we attach to, who we spend time with, how we invest our energy, what behaviour we

> accept from others, what fears and doubts we let go of, and how we respond to tests from the universe. The choices you make determine who you become and what you manifest into your life.

If you are on your manifesting journey, become aware of tests. When they present themselves to you, do not allow them to lower your vibration and take you off course. Use them to strengthen your manifesting power by showing the universe that you value yourself and that you believe you are worthy of receiving abundance into your life. Stand up for yourself when you need to, say no to enticing opportunities if they don't fill all the requirements, stay strong when faced with rejection and trust that everything will work out just as it is supposed to.

One of my favourite quotes is 'Sometimes you win, sometimes you learn.' It reminds me that everything has the potential to teach us something valuable. Instead of seeing things as 'going wrong' or 'going right', you can see everything as an opportunity for learning, expansion and growth. That is why this step is my personal favourite: when you are able to see challenges as nothing more than tests that you can overcome, you begin to let go of so much unnecessary stress and instead begin to ride the waves of life with so much more ease and fluidity. That ease enables you to raise your vibe and empowers you to manifest even more powerfully and effortlessly.

STEP 5

EMBRACE GRATITUDE (WITHOUT CAVEATS)

'A grateful heart is a magnet for miracles.'

UNKNOWN AUTHOR

Back in the introduction to this book, I explained that different emotions have different vibrational frequencies. Emotions such as shame, anger, jealousy and guilt all have a low-vibrational frequency. On the other hand, emotions such as joy, happiness, love, peace, contentment and appreciation all have a high-vibrational frequency. The universe does not really hear our thoughts; it responds to the frequencies that those thoughts create: **we attract what we feel**.

When I first learned that our emotions had the power to shape our reality, I instinctively knew just how true it was. I started to recall countless occasions when I had experienced low-vibe emotions (such as anger, sadness and despair) and, as a result, I had manifested negative situations into my life. In fact, although I didn't admit this to myself at the time, I constantly manifested negative situations into my life to support my belief that I was unworthy and that life was unfair. I would play out worst-case scenarios in my head, and then when they happened in real life I would say, 'I knew this was going to happen.' For example, when I was twenty-two, I left my first nine-to-five job, working at Diageo, and decided to set up something on my own. I'd always known that I wanted to help empower women so I thought that perhaps I could use my love of fashion to help women present themselves in a way that made them feel their most confident. So, I decided to try and become a 'fashion stylist'. I started to approach potential clients (basically, my friends and acquaintances) to ask if I could help re-vamp their wardrobes, but whenever I reached out to them I heard my inner voice saying, 'They're never going to say yes because they know you are not good enough.' Then, when they replied, politely declining my offer, the voice would say, 'I told you so.' Suffice it to say that my career as a 'stylist' never took off, and in two years I only managed to acquire one single paying client before I decided to give it up altogether. The sole reason for this lay in my own lack of self-worth and the constant attachment to low-vibe emotions that were holding me back. I simply didn't have the self-belief or the fearlessness to take action or to move forward when faced with obstacles. This is just one example, but in truth I spent an entire decade searching for evidence that I was a failure who was destined for unhappiness. Now, I can see that I was responsible for keeping myself trapped in that stagnant space for so long. **The power to manifest had always been in me, but I'd been using it in the wrong direction.**

Can you think of a time when you've been angry, jealous or fearful and then you have manifested something negative into your life? Or have you ever had one of those mornings when you've woken up late and felt tired and grouchy? You wake up in that flat, low-vibe mood and you just can't shake it. You sit down for breakfast and spill your coffee everywhere, you leave the house and, halfway to the station, you remember that you've left your phone at home so you go back to get it and miss your train, then you get a text from your friend cancelling a meet-up later that you've been looking forward to. You just have one of those days where you literally say, 'Ugh, it's just one of those days!' If you really think about it, do you believe it's a coincidence that those things so often happen in succession like that? Recently, I was feeling angry with myself about a mistake I had made at work and, as I walked out of the room, I stubbed my toe on the door, and I actually laughed to myself. It felt like a little message from the universe that said, 'Hey, don't forget I'm always watching you.' **Our vibe matters.**

When I first understood the power that we have not only to draw abundance to us but to attract negativity to us, too, I panicked. Perhaps you are reading this and panicking a little, too. You might be thinking, 'Does that mean every time I feel angry I will attract something bad to me? Or on the days I wake up feeling flat something terrible will happen to me? I can't be expected to be "high vibe" all the time, can I?' No, of course you can't be expected to, and it is important that we do give ourselves space to feel, validate, accept and honour the full spectrum of emotions. So, what do we do when we feel overwhelmed with a low-vibe feeling? **We use gratitude.**

Gratitude is defined as a feeling of appreciation, and this feeling has an extremely high vibrational frequency. Gratitude is one of the most powerful emotional tools we have at our disposal and when we understand how to practise it we can use it to instantly pull ourselves out of any low-vibe experience, to change our state, to shift our vibration and to completely unleash the abundance of the universe. On a day where we feel flat, low, angry, jealous, resentful or fearful, we can turn to gratitude to help us. We can take a moment to pause, to find stillness, and then to cultivate and embrace gratitude to override any low-vibe emotion we are experiencing.

THREE CATEGORIES OF GRATITUDE

Gratitude for the self

These are things that you can appreciate about yourself, e.g. I am grateful for my strength, I am grateful for my health, I am grateful for my mind.

Gratitude for your life

These are the things in your life that you appreciate, e.g. I am grateful for my job, I am grateful for my family and friends, I am grateful for where I live.

Gratitude for the world

These are the things you feel grateful for that are universal to us all, e.g. I am grateful for the sunshine, I am grateful for connection, I am grateful for the ability to travel and experience new cultures.

You can use these three categories to help guide you in practising and cultivating gratitude into your life.

Note: Some days you might find that, in the midst of a particularly intense feeling of fear, sadness or anger, you are unable to feel gratitude for yourself or for the things in your life. That is why I have laid out three categories of gratitude for you, so that you can always find something that you can feel grateful for: if you are struggling to feel grateful for your own life today, focus on your gratitude for something universal. Just remember: there is *always* something to be grateful for, if you take the time to focus on it.

When we feel grateful for the things we currently have, we feel content, present and at peace. We raise our vibe instantly. Let me show you . . . Take a second now to think of one thing you feel truly grateful for. Think about it, visualize it clearly and allow the feeling of gratitude to really flow through your body. Do you notice how, when you think about something that you're truly grateful for, your body physically shifts? Your muscles start to relax, you may begin to smile unconsciously and you feel immediately calmer.

About a month after I first discovered manifesting I came across Dr Joe Dispenza. I heard him speak on a podcast with Gwyneth Paltrow and as soon as it had finished I typed his name into YouTube and sat listening intently to him talk in countless videos. I found his knowledge and his passion so insightful and *so* inspiring. But there was one finding he shared that really stuck with me, one that influenced my own manifesting journey from that moment on: studies have found that, in just four days, transforming your fear to 'gratitude, appreciation and kindness for just ten minutes a day, three times a day, can strengthen your immune system by fifty per cent'. How incredible is that? Replacing your fears and doubts with gratitude can actually change your physiology, change the behaviour of your cells, shift your vibrational frequency and even help to protect you against disease. This was a massive wake-up call for me. It was scientific evidence of the incredible power of our minds – the power that we have to change our reality – and it was evidence of the immense power of gratitude. This is what manifesting really became to me from that moment: the joining of science and wisdom. The understanding that we can use our minds to shift our energy, to raise our vibrational frequency and then change our reality. And gratitude was very much at the core of it.

In that moment, it all started to make sense. I looked back at my own journey and my own behaviour up until then. If I was honest with myself, I had never embraced *true* gratitude. I was always complaining about what I didn't have, looking at others wishing I had what they had, or waiting for something or someone to come into my life and magically make me happy. Perhaps you know what I mean . . . How many times have you thought, 'I'll be happy when . . . ' or 'If I had what they had, then I'd be happy?' This pattern of thinking is so limiting because it keeps us locked in a scarcity mindset. It sends a message to the universe that says, 'My life is lacking,' or 'I don't have enough,' and so that is what the universe will continue to give you: lack and scarcity. But it limits you in another way, too: waiting for something or someone to make you feel a certain way gives away your own inner power. It prevents you from taking responsibility for your own happiness.

> TO MANIFEST, WE HAVE TO FIRST UNDERSTAND THAT WE ARE THE CURATORS, THE ARCHITECTS AND THE CONDUCTORS OF OUR LIVES AND OUR DESTINY.

At the time, though, if you'd asked me, 'Are you a grateful person?', I would have said, 'Yes, absolutely.' I really believed that I was, but then I would say things like 'I know I'm lucky in so many ways, but if I was in a relationship, I'd be so much happier.' I was always attaching caveats to my gratitude, and this is what was preventing me from feeling and experiencing *true* gratitude.

I began to realize that people were almost always attaching caveats to their gratitude. They'd say something like 'I love my house, but I can't wait to be somewhere with more space,' or 'I love my job, but it would be so much better if I was paid more,' or 'It's great I made some sales today, but I was hoping to have sold out by now.' These caveats are attached so casually and automatically that most people are not even aware that they are using them.

I started to ask myself why we always attach caveats to our gratitude. I believe that one of the reasons is because many of us hold a subconscious fear that if we are completely happy with what we have, then we won't ever strive for more. For example, if we have complete gratitude for our current salary, won't that stop us feeling motivated to work towards a promotion? Or if we are totally happy with the house we live in, doesn't that mean we will never end up experiencing life somewhere new?

There is an underlying belief that true and full gratitude comes at the expense of drive, motivation and our ability to progress. I am here to remove that fear for you: true gratitude, without caveats, does not hold you back. It is, in fact, an integral part of your manifesting journey.

> **You have to be clear in your vision and about where you want to go while simultaneously being entirely grateful for all that you currently have: this is what I call the manifesting sweet spot.**

I thought I'd tell you a little story of how I used this step myself to manifest my current home.

When I had just discovered that I was ten weeks pregnant with my son, I had no career, I was making very little money and I had no idea what I was going to do with my life. I had manifested meeting Wade a few months previously, but I was not prepared for what happened next: falling pregnant. I'd been living in a beautiful apartment which I could no longer afford, and Wade and I had nowhere to go. My dad very kindly said we could live in his apartment in Waterloo. I walked into an extremely run-down flat which had been left in a complete mess by the previous tenants and I was immediately hit by this foul smell. The decor was the same as it was when it had been purchased over twenty-two years ago, but now there was a hole in the door, marks all over the walls, mould covering the tiles in the bathroom and the shower did little more than dribble water. I thought, 'I am twenty-eight years old, having a baby with a man I met just three months ago, and this is nothing like the life I imagined for myself: jobless, pregnant and living in this neglected apartment.' I'd wanted to manifest a glamorous life, I thought. This was *not* glamorous. I was a total brat about it all. I was always complaining about the space, and I would lie down, trying to imagine where I would be next, thinking that visualizing it would be enough to manifest it. I cringe now, thinking back on it.

But as time went on and my baby bump grew bigger, I started getting into 'nesting mode', so I redecorated the apartment, slowly but surely, sold all the stuff I no longer had space for at car-boot sales and really started to make it a home, ready for Wolfe's arrival. I began to like it more, but I was still saying to myself, 'This is good for now, *I guess.*' I was trying to be grateful, because I knew that I should be, but I wasn't truly embracing it.

Then the Covid-19 pandemic hit and Prime Minister Boris Johnson announced that we must all now 'stay at home to save lives'. The home I had once resented moving into became my sanctuary. It became my home, my office, my gym and my play area. I fell totally in love with it. I had so much time to reflect and, as if a penny had dropped, I finally thought to myself, 'I am so, so lucky to have a roof over my head. I love the home I have made for my little family. I am ridiculously fortunate to be living in an apartment that my dad worked so hard to buy. I am genuinely so happy and content to be here.' I meant it, from the bottom of my heart. I felt immense gratitude fill me up. Then, on one of our many daily lockdown walks, Wade asked me, 'What does your dream home look like?' I described an island kitchen with a double-door fridge and marble worktops and a glorious bath to soak in. My dream home. The next day, I went on Instagram and saw a friend upload a video of herself working out in her home, *with an island kitchen behind her.* I messaged her and said, 'Wow, your house is so beautiful.' She replied a minute later, saying, 'Wanna buy it?' I jokingly replied, 'Lol, how much?' The timing had aligned in the most incredible way and the flat, which should have been way out of my price range, was being hugely undersold at a figure I could actually afford. By now, I had carved out my own career and I was working extremely hard (aka aligning my behaviour and taking action!), but I knew in my heart that it was my sincere gratitude for what

I already had that had led me to manifest my dream home in just a matter of days.

When you want to manifest something into your life, you must be clear in your vision, remove your fear and doubt, align your behaviour, overcome tests from the universe and then embrace gratitude without caveats for all that you currently have. Allow that feeling of appreciation to shift your entire state of being. Feel the gratitude raise your vibe and keep you in an abundant mindset.

> THE BEAUTY OF THE WORLD CAN ONLY BE EXPERIENCED BY SOMEONE WHO IS WILLING TO SEE IT.

If you are willing to see all the beauty and love and abundance that are already present in your life, you will effortlessly attract more beauty, more love and more abundance to you.

To live in 'an attitude of gratitude', we must cultivate it so that it becomes part of our essence. We must practise it over and over again in order to begin to rewire our neurological pathways so that we automatically focus on all the good in our lives rather than the bad. If you do this, you will change your natural state, redirect your attention to abundance and allow your manifesting process to become effortless. **Remember that where attention goes, energy flows.** So, focus on what is good, and more good will come to you.

Here are some things you can do to cultivate and embrace gratitude (without caveats).

JOURNALING

I absolutely love journaling and it is a self-development tool that I come back to again and again. Consistent gratitude journaling can be used to retrain your brain on a neurological level to focus on the good in your life, making this a powerful manifesting practice.

Here are two ways to practise gratitude journaling.

Technique 1: Gratitude lists

Every night, or every morning, write down fifteen things you are grateful for. I like to choose five things from each of the three gratitude categories above. So, I start with five things that I am grateful for about myself (e.g. I am grateful for my resilience), then five things that I am grateful for that happened in the day (e.g. I am grateful for the time I spent with my baby boy) and, finally, five things that I am grateful for in the world (e.g. I am grateful for the sound of the ocean).

Technique 2: Positivity journal

This is my favourite journaling practice and one that I developed for myself last year.

At the end of each day, write down *every single good thing* that happened to you that day, from the moment you woke up to the moment you got into bed. I really mean *everything*: if the sun was shining, if a stranger smiled at you, if a friend sent you a thoughtful message, or if you saw a meme on social media that made you laugh. Write it all down in chronological order.

So often, the day can pass us by and we forget how many beautiful moments we have experienced. They can go totally unnoticed and unappreciated. We can even assume that a whole day was 'bad' just because of one bad moment within it. But when we sit down to recollect all the good that we experienced we soon see that each and every day is filled with so much to be thankful for.

After committing to completing your positivity journaling daily, your mind will begin to automatically look out for all the beautiful moments and opportunities that each day brings. After a couple of weeks, you might suddenly find yourself walking along the street saying to yourself, 'Wow, what a stunning building,' having finally noticed the incredible architecture that you have walked past mindlessly every day up until then. Or you might have a new-found appreciation for the cup of tea your partner brings you in bed every morning, or for the kind smile the receptionist at your office gives you when you walk in each morning. You will simply begin to notice more of the good around you, and in turn you will raise your vibe throughout the day, every day.

I created this practice for myself when I found myself in a career rut last year. I was suffering from a bout of imposter syndrome and I was feeling really stuck with some of my desired manifestations. I had been given a notebook as a gift and on the front of it was written 'Positivity' so I decided to turn it into my 'positivity journal' to shift me out of the funk I was in. I wrote in it every night for two weeks. At the end of the two weeks, I had a breakthrough and one of my visions came to life: to write about manifesting for British *Vogue*. I was in the middle of doing an online workout (when all my best ideas seem come to me) and I heard an inner voice saying, 'If you really want to contribute to *Vogue*, you need to take action. Step outside your comfort zone and send the email. The worst that will happen is that they say no.' So, with my high-vibrational state of gratitude driving me forward, I paused my Pilates class and wrote an email to the digital editor, Kerry McDermott, and asked her if there was any chance that I could write about manifesting for the online magazine. She replied a couple of hours later, saying, 'As it happens, I commissioned an article to be written about manifesting last week and it's being submitted tomorrow. I'll put you in touch with the writer, Giselle La Pompe-Moore, and you can be involved too.' I had emailed her just in time. If I had not taken action when the inspiration came to me, I would have missed the opportunity. It was a brilliant demonstration of manifesting in action: I'd had the vision of writing for *Vogue*, I used gratitude to pull me out of my self-doubt, then I released any fear or limiting beliefs that I wasn't worthy of being in *Vogue* by aligning my behaviour and taking action. I cannot tell you how immensely proud I felt when I saw the article: my younger self was screaming inside!

REEL OFF THE GOOD

Whenever you find yourself in a low-vibe funk like the one I describe above, allow gratitude to raise you back up by using this simple technique which you can do anywhere. Simply take a moment to pause and then, without stopping to think about it, reel off everything you feel grateful for until you feel something within yourself shift. You can do this by writing things down on the notes app on your phone, saying them out loud to yourself or to a friend, or writing them in your journal.

I use this technique any time I feel myself getting upset or annoyed, or if I wake up feeling a bit 'off'. It only takes a couple of minutes, which makes it a simple yet effective gratitude practice. Just reel off all the good.

SWITCH 'I *HAVE* TO DO IT' FOR 'I *GET* TO DO IT'

I remember going to one of my first spin classes in London, at a studio aptly called Psycle. The session was reaching its climax: I was sweating, my breath was short, my legs were getting tired and heavy and all I could think about was how much I wanted the experience to be over. Then, as if he was reading my mind, the trainer shouted to the class through his microphone, 'Remember: you don't *have* to be here, you *get* to be here!' It was a lightbulb moment for me. I had chosen to be there – no one had forced me on to the bike. In fact, every single person who was in that class got to be there because they were fortunate enough to have a healthy body that allowed them to pedal with their legs, they were lucky enough to live somewhere that offered the class, and they were in a privileged enough position to be able to afford to book themselves a spot. In that moment of physical exhaustion, there was so much to be grateful for when I stopped to consider it, so why was I now wishing the experience away? That trainer totally shifted my perspective: he instantly brought me back to the present moment and I felt immense gratitude fill me up.

This perspective shift became a powerful gratitude tool that I now encourage people to use every day. How many times have you said, 'I have to work out today,' or 'I have to go to work,' or 'I have to go see my parents,' or 'I have to study,' or 'I have to cook dinner for the kids again'? Using this language implies that you have no choice and that you are being forced into something. It takes away the opportunity for us to feel grateful and it implies that we don't have the power to choose. When you make the simple language switch and instead say, 'I get to exercise today,' or 'I get to go to work today,' or 'I get to see my parents,' or 'I get to study,' or 'I get to cook dinner for the kids,' you automatically shift yourself into a state of appreciation. This is because when we say 'I get to' we remind ourselves that some do not: we remind ourselves, consciously and subconsciously, how fortunate we are that we are able to move our bodies, to see our loved ones and to live the life that we do.

PRACTISE MINDFULNESS

How many times a day do you say, 'I can't wait for . . .' or 'I will be so happy when . . .'? It's something that most of us do automatically, me included. I regularly catch myself sitting at lunch thinking about what I am going to have for dinner, or spending hours thinking about how excited I am for a manifestation to come through: 'It's going to feel so incredible when . . .' We say these things with good intentions: it feels good to be excited about something and it is fun to daydream about what we want to manifest. In fact, I regularly advise people to have something in mind to look forward to and, of course, knowing what you want and where you want to be in the future is the first step of manifesting. **The problems begin when we start to focus on the future at the expense of living in a mindful way.** Looking to the future too often (regardless of whether it is a positive or a negative future we're imagining) prevents us from living in the present moment, and when we are not present we cannot fully embrace gratitude. This is one of the reasons that I advise people to put their vision boards away after they've made them.

To cultivate gratitude, we must practise training ourselves to be more mindful. Whatever you are doing, make a conscious effort to be 100 per cent there. For example, when you are in the office, be 100 per cent there; when you are with your family, be 100 per cent with them; when you are in the gym, be 100 per cent in it. Doing this will not only enrich all your experiences and reduce the stress that accompanies split-focus, it will also help you to train your mind to live more mindfully. Every time you catch yourself losing focus and find that your mind is distracting you from where you currently are, pull yourself back to the moment. Focus your attention on how you currently feel and what you can see and hear and focus your attention on the people you are with.

Another way to practise more mindful living is to incorporate meditation into your daily routine. Meditation is a practice of stillness and presence and, just in the same way you train your abdominal muscles to be strong, you can train your mind to be more mindful. If you're new to meditation, I suggest beginning by following guided meditations, starting with just five minutes then working your way up to a longer meditation practice when you feel ready. When entering the world of meditation, which is filled with incredible physical, mental and spiritual benefits, be careful not to judge your practice or to expect to find stillness straight away. The idea that when we meditate we should be void of all thoughts is a meditation myth! The aim is not to empty our minds entirely but to learn to observe our thoughts without attaching to them. Meditation is the practice of mindful awareness, using stillness and breath to quieten our minds.

I highly recommend incorporating some form of meditation into your daily routine, making it one of your high-vibe, self-love practices. For me, daily meditation practice is non-negotiable; it helps me to slow down my mind, opens up space for creativity and ideas to come to me and allows me to increase my capacity for gratitude by strengthening my ability to live mindfully. It is an integral part of my own manifesting processes and I always make time for it: some days I simply breathe mindfully for five minutes and other days I delve into a thirty-minute meditative manifesting visualization before bed.

A selection of guided meditations, including a manifesting meditation, is available on my website: www.roxienafousi.com

NOTICE THE LITTLE THINGS

As we begin to live more mindfully, we give ourselves more opportunity to notice all the little things in our lives that can evoke those powerful high-vibe feelings of appreciation.

Things that might have previously gone unnoticed can now become an anchor for that contented, joyful feeling. These little things are otherwise known as *life's small pleasures*. Start to really pay attention to them, sit with them, feel them and experience them fully. In doing so, you keep bringing yourself back to gratitude, constantly strengthening your manifesting power.

LIFE'S SMALL PLEASURES

Examples: the smell of freshly brewed coffee, getting into a bed with newly laundered sheets, the sound of birds in the morning, the feeling of warm wind on your face, quenching your thirst with ice-cold water, the sound of the ocean, morning sunlight, tidying up, lighting a candle, flowers, the smell of just-cut grass, a smile from a passer-by . . .

Write down ten of your favourite small pleasures:

1. ....
....
2. ....
....
3. ....
....
4. ....
....
5. ....
....
6. ....
....
7. ....
....
8. ....
....
9. ....
....
10. ....
....

On the road to manifesting your dreams, don't forget to enjoy the journey that takes you there. Pay attention to the small, simple joys of life and be present in each day. Remember: a grateful heart is a magnet for miracles.

MANIFEST

STEP 6

TURN ENVY INTO INSPIRATION

ENVY: A FEELING OF DISCONTENTED
OR RESENTFUL LONGING AROUSED
BY SOMEONE ELSE'S POSSESSIONS,
QUALITIES, OR LUCK (*OXFORD
ENGLISH DICTIONARY*)

Envy is a low-vibrational emotion that stems from a scarcity mindset. Your envy says to the universe, 'When I see someone else with something that I want, I feel resentful because I don't believe that I can have it for myself.'

INSPIRATION: A SUDDEN FEELING
OF ENTHUSIASM, OR A NEW IDEA
THAT HELPS YOU TO DO OR CREATE
SOMETHING (*MACMILLAN
DICTIONARY*)

Inspiration is a high-vibrational feeling that stems from an abundance mindset. Seeing something that you desire and feeling inspired by it says to the universe, 'I believe there is enough for everyone, and I believe that I can have it too.'

Envy is one of those emotions you can physically feel rise up from within you. I often feel it in the pit of my stomach: it comes on like a wave of panic followed by a subtle lingering of frustration, anger and sadness all in one. Sometimes envy hits us right in the face, for example when a colleague gets the job promotion we applied for, or when we see a loved-up couple kissing at the traffic lights the day after our fiancé dumped us after seven seemingly blissful years. But more often than not envy is much more insidious in nature: it quietly creeps up on us, embeds itself within us and leaves us feeling discontented and dissatisfied with our lives without us even understanding why. While we mindlessly scroll through our social media feeds, our subconscious is being bombarded with images of perfection, with opportunities for comparison, with things we wish we had and with reasons to feel that our life is just not as good as somebody else's.

Social media is a billion-dollar industry that is literally driven by envy: it actively encourages us to compare ourselves to others so that we buy what they have, while simultaneously encouraging us to post our own envy-inducing images to get us enough 'likes' or 'comments' to feel validated.

> HOW OFTEN DO YOU COME OFF SOCIAL MEDIA FEELING JUST A LITTLE BIT WORSE ABOUT YOURSELF AND YOUR LIFE THAN YOU DID BEFORE YOU WENT ON?

A woman in one of my group coaching sessions said that over the last couple of months she had been dreading her Friday and Saturday evenings. When I asked her why, she said that it was because every weekend she would go on social media and see people out and about, socializing, going to bars, restaurants or parties, and that this would always make her feel jealous. The other women in the group all nodded along; they could relate to her experience. I asked her a simple question: 'Do you actually want to go out every weekend?' She said, 'Yes, of course I do.' Then I gently said, 'Well, why do you choose to stay in? Because, if you really wanted to go out, you could surely find a way to do that?' You could see the realization coming over her face as she thought about it. Of course, if she *really* wanted to, one of her friends would happily go out with her. Then she said, 'Actually, I guess, although I enjoy going out for special occasions, on the whole I just love spending the evenings getting a delicious take-away, watching a movie, putting on a face mask and having the chance to reset after a busy week at work.' Then she explained that she really valued waking up fresh on Sundays because that was when she met up with her weekly running club. In that moment she realized that social media was making her feel envious of something she didn't even want.

Social media is a playground for comparison and a fertile land for envy to grow in. We are shown endless images of who we think we should be or what our lives should look like. Whether it's being constantly presented with the 'perfect' body, the dream home, a successful business, a heavenly holiday or an idyllic family, the 'dream' life is always being sold to us at the expense of our appreciation of our own.

This endless portrayal of the 'perfect life' can trigger envy all day long if we allow it to. But the ironic thing about it all is that we are envious of things that aren't even real. So much of the content that we see online is staged, pre-planned, edited, airbrushed and fine-tuned for the sole purpose of making it look appealing and *enviable*. I've seen friends uploading perfect-couple selfies minutes after calling me to tell me they are about leave their partner because their toxic relationship has become so unbearable, and I've called friends to say, 'Oh my goodness, your holiday looked just incredible,' only for them to tell me that it was, in fact, the holiday from hell. We are shown a masked reality, a mirage, and we continue striving for them seemingly unaware that in doing so, we are merely searching for a pot of gold at the end of the rainbow.

My own relationship with social media was completely toxic for many years. It was a place where I would go just to prove to myself that I was not enough. As I battled silently with depression, I would look at people on the internet posting pictures of themselves smiling, laughing, dancing, as if care-free, and the envy that overcame me was painful. I desperately wanted to feel that effortless joy they appeared to possess and I almost resented everyone else who seemed to be able to live life without immense sadness and debilitating self-loathing. My depression went hand in hand with my hedonistic partying phase and during that time I was also desperate to be part of the 'cool' social scene in London. I thought that if I could just be invited to the *Love* magazine Fashion Week party, I would finally feel validated. Or if I got a seat at the British Fashion Awards, I might feel worthy at last. Then, inevitably, Fashion Week or the Fashion Awards would come around and no invitation would come through the door. I would sit at home, open up Instagram, see everyone uploading their fabulous pictures and even more fabulous outfits and that familiar feeling of envy would take me over again. It was the envy that said to me, 'You're not as good as them,' the envy that kept me, my self-worth and my vibe at a permanently low level. As I stared at my phone I felt just as I had done for the majority of my life, that I was on the outside looking in. Just as I was harming my body with drugs, alcohol and cigarettes, I was harming my mind by deliberately exposing myself to things I knew would support my belief that I wasn't enough.

We all know that we can self-sabotage with excessive drinking, shopping beyond our means, staying in toxic relationships and procrastinating on important tasks, but we can use social media to self-sabotage, too. I have one friend who just can't seem to stop herself looking at her ex-boyfriend's new partner's profile. She stalks her page every day; it has become a part of her evening routine. She looks at her photos, makes assumptions about what her life must be like, then begins the comparison game, allowing the inevitable feelings of envy to take hold. She knows the harm it is doing to her self-esteem, but she can't seem to stop herself.

My advice? Monitor and manage your social media usage. I should add a disclaimer here: I do actually love social media. All the platforms have so much to offer and, if used correctly, social media can inspire, motivate, connect and entertain us in the most wonderful ways. But in order to be able to enjoy all its benefits without the constant negative triggers, I advise you to do two things:

1. Curate your feed: Mute or unfollow people whose posts don't make you feel good or if you know they trigger you. You can always unmute them when you feel that you are able to follow them and see their content from a healthier perspective (that is, when you feel more confident in yourself). Then, choose to follow people who you find engaging, inspiring or relatable so you can see more of their content on your feeds.

2. Scroll mindfully: When you're on an app, be mindful and present so that you aren't aimlessly scrolling and allowing unwanted triggers or information to be taken in without your full awareness. By being mindful you will allow yourself to pay more attention to how certain things make you feel, so if you do feel triggered you can acknowledge it and then begin to process it.

It is not only when we are on social media that we feel envious. In fact, more often than not we can feel envy much more deeply and intensely in relation to the people closest to us.

Has a friend ever told you about the surprise holiday their partner booked them, or how they're feeling the best they have ever felt, and even though you want to be nothing but happy for them, you can't help but feel jealous and envious? Or have you ever found yourself caught in sibling rivalry, stuck in a dynamic of constant arguing, and, deep down, you know that it's only because you are jealous of how much more attention you feel they get from your parents?

It can feel really confusing when we feel jealous of the people we love. We ask ourselves, 'If I really love this person, and if I am a good friend to them, how can I be jealous of them?' Cue shame, guilt and self-judgement. The self-judgement can be so uncomfortable that it can cause us to try to deny our envy entirely. Have you ever denied your envy and reframed it to say something like 'I just don't like her,' or 'I never liked her,' or 'I would actually hate to have what she has?' **But no good can come from denied envy.** When envy is buried, we trap the low-vibe emotions within us and they feed into our insecurities and low self-worth, which serves only to keep us further from our manifestation.

We all know that envy, especially when it is buried deep down, can cause people to act in ways that are unkind and unfair and sometimes just straight-up cruel. How many times have you been told that the reason someone is being nasty or rude to you is because they are secretly jealous? If we repeatedly deny our envy, its insidious nature strengthens. We transfer our envy and pass it on as judgement of others. It's a horrible cycle. The most compassionate thing we can do for ourselves, and for those around us, is to first and foremost acknowledge how we are really feeling. Rather than push those feelings aside or suppress them, allow them to teach you something. For example, if you see someone with unwavering confidence walk into a room, instead of immediately passing judgement and saying something like 'She's so arrogant,' maybe ask yourself if you admire and desire that confidence for yourself. Or if you see a couple kissing at a table beside you and you are about to judge their public display of affection, perhaps ask yourself, 'Am I only passing judgement because I wish to be in a loving, passionate relationship?'

With some honest self-reflection, you can see your envy, acknowledge it and allow it to show you what you want and feel that you need more of in your life. Once we begin to recognize and embrace our feelings, rather than denying and judging them, we open up space to listen to what our feelings are telling us. However, before we do that, I thought it might be worth explaining *why* we judge our envy so intensely.

I'm going to tell you a story you have probably heard before. It is the story of Snow White. In this story, the wicked queen asks the magic mirror, 'Who is the fairest of them all?' When she sees that the reflection in the mirror is not of herself but of Snow White, her jealousy takes over. It drives her to order her loyal huntsman to kill the kind and beautiful Snow White. In this story, envy is portrayed to us as it always is: as something evil. In almost all children's films and fairy tales there is a jealous villain (think Scar in *The Lion King*, the ugly stepsisters in *Cinderella* or Jaffar in *Aladdin*). We read these stories and watch these films as children, and so when we grow up and begin to experience feelings of jealousy ourselves, we panic. We attach shame to our envy because we associate it with evil.

But envy is not evil in itself. It is simply an emotion we feel when we are faced with something that makes us question our own self-worth. Envy does not always rear its head as the green-eyed monster we so often perceive it to be. No, more often than not, envy is simply a representation of our fear – a fear that we might lose something we love and are emotionally and energetically invested in. We fear that if someone else has something, we will somehow lose out (hello, scarcity mindset). Anyone who has ever started their own business will know what I mean: as we embark on something new that requires immense energy and investment, we can become hypersensitive to the success of others doing something similar to us.

I have a friend who had just become a personal trainer. Through-out the whole process of studying to get her qualification, she was so excited, optimistic and energized by the idea of it, and she would always look at other trainers for inspiration and motiva-tion. But the moment she got her certification, envy took hold. She would text me, saying, 'Did you see that so-and-so is now a personal trainer too? I can't believe it.' She became obsessed with looking at the other trainers in the area and comparing herself with them. But it wasn't really envy, it was fear. She was afraid that after investing so much money and time into training for this, she might not acquire the number of clients she desired. The fear was driving her envy and it was blocking her from stepping into her power. She needed to first recognize that her envy was a symptom of her fear and then she needed to begin healing her own insecurities.

If envy is driven by fear, then that must mean we can use it to direct us to whatever limiting beliefs, insecurities or doubts are still blocking us from our manifestation.

The most effective way, then, to let go of envy, is to continu-ously work to remove the fear and doubt that is driving it. But as I mentioned in Step 2: Remove Fear and Doubt (see page 29), that process is ongoing. In the meantime, what can we do so that the low-vibe emotion doesn't linger and block us from moving forward in our manifesting journey?

We can turn our envy into inspiration.

Inspiration is the antithesis of envy. While envy comes from the low-vibe place of scarcity, inspiration is high vibe and comes from a place of abundance. The panic that rises up when we feel jealous of someone is really just panic that their success will take away from our own opportunities. Envy says, 'There is not enough,' while inspiration says, 'There is an end-less supply.'

Whenever we experience envy, we have an opportunity to reframe our thinking and choose an inspired perspective that will push us closer towards our dreams.

> ENVIOUS THOUGHT: 'THIS IS
> SOMETHING THAT THEY HAVE, AND I
> CAN'T HAVE.'
> INSPIRED THOUGHT: 'THIS IS
> SOMETHING THAT THEY HAVE AND
> THAT I WOULD LIKE FOR MYSELF,
> TOO.'

I often have people coming to me wanting to manifest a relationship. The same people will nearly always tell me that when they see their friends in relationships, getting married or starting families, they really struggle to be happy for them. They see it as another reminder of how 'far behind' they are on their own journey and even use phrases like 'It's so unfair.' I remind them that this feeling of envy comes from a mindset that there isn't enough love to go around and this is actively blocking them from attracting their soulmate into their life. I encourage them to instead look at their friends' relationships and turn their envy into inspiration by saying something like 'I love seeing two people so happy together. It is so beautiful to watch, and I am so excited to experience that for myself when the time is right.' It is such a simple mindset shift, but such an effective one.

Another example of where you can turn your envy into inspiration might be this. Imagine you bump into an old friend and you decide to go for a coffee and catch up. She tells you that after leaving school she started her own very successful tech business then sold it, enabling her to travel around the world for the last twelve months – hence her glowing, sun-kissed complexion. Notice how you feel physically, emotionally and mentally in response to that information. Do you feel that wave of panic culminating in the feelings of subtle sadness, discontentment and frustration that I described earlier? If so, first validate your experience by saying to yourself, 'Hearing this has made me feel jealous/envious.' Then remove judgement and replace it with self-love, compassion and kindness, remembering that it's OK to feel that way. When you have done that, take the empowering decision to **turn your envy into inspiration**. You could choose an inspired thought, such as 'I am so happy to see someone who has built a career for themselves that gave them the freedom to pursue their passion. Perhaps I will begin to explore how I can do this for myself.' You can then use their success to inspire your own vision of what you want to manifest.

Remember: We live in a society where we see the media constantly tearing people down with provocative head-lines that encourage trolling and judgement. This enables envy-driven behaviour. It normalizes judging and criticizing others for their actions. It gives people an opportunity to express their envy in a way that feels acceptable, and this is a dangerous cycle for everyone. We have to start to call out envy whenever it begins to surface. I have definitely found that group get-togethers or WhatsApp chats can easily turn to a gossip-fest that is fuelled by jealousy. It usually doesn't take long for groups of friends to unite against one other person and talk negatively about them and their choices. This kind of behaviour is so low-vibe, and not only is it seriously unkind and a total waste of time, it also sabotages our own manifesting power. It is almost always driven by envy, even if we don't like to admit it. When you see it happening, call it out or, at the very least, step away from these kinds of toxic conversations.

Tearing other people down is low vibe. Building people up is high vibe.

> To support other people, to build them up, to cele-
> brate them, to help them, to encourage them: that
> comes from a place of self-love and high self-worth. It
> shows the universe that you are not threatened by the
> success of others, you are inspired by it. That inspira-
> tion will drive you to your manifestation. If you keep
> putting that loving, magnetic and magical energy out
> into the universe, you will receive abundance. Building
> a community of love, connection and complete non-
> judgement is something I am always championing and
> encouraging, not least because it helps us all on our
> own manifesting journeys.

Turning envy into inspiration will not only pull you from low
vibe to high vibe, it will also help you to gain more clarity on
what you want to add to your vision board and it can help you
to bring a visualization to life. For example, let's say you want to
manifest a winter wedding. While you may already feel strongly
that this is what you want, it might only be when you attend a
winter wedding and see it through your own eyes that you're
really able to visualize it clearly. Then, when you next go to do
a visualization meditation or make your vision board, you will
have a much more enriched and vivid image in your mind.

Turning envy into inspiration is a great tool to use when scrolling through social media, too. For example, if you are scrolling
through your Instagram feed and see someone at a newly
opened restaurant eating a delicious meal with a group of
friends and you sense an 'envy signal', take a second to pause,
acknowledge it and then turn the envy into inspiration by saying, 'This is a place I want to go, I'll add it to my list of places
to book. I can't wait to experience it for myself.' Use those holiday pictures, couple selfies or interior pictures that come up on

your feed to help you visualize the things you desire. Be inspired by the things you see and actively say to yourself, 'This is something I want. This is something I know I deserve. This is what I am going to manifest.'

When we are inspired by other people's accomplishments or experiences we show the universe that we believe the world has more than enough love, happiness and success to go around. And so that is what we will attract: more love, more happiness, more success.

I use this tool myself all the time: there are thousands and thousands of coaches, mentors, teachers and writers out there, and self-development is a fast-growing industry. If I were to compare myself to everyone else who does something similar to me, or if I allowed myself to feel envious of other people's success, I would be forever stuck in a scarcity mindset. I would be triggered every single time I saw another person upload a self-development post, write for a magazine, host a workshop or release a book. Imagine how low my vibe would be if I allowed myself to sit in that space and how suffocating that envy would be! Instead, I choose to actively celebrate the success of others in my industry and I look to them with an honest feeling of awe and inspiration for all the wonderful things they do. I do this because I know, in my heart, that for the thousands of brilliant people out there coaching, teaching and writing, there are a million more people wanting to learn and be helped on their personal-development journeys. I see and believe in the abundance of opportunities to help, inspire and motivate others and so abundance comes to me in return. I don't want to be the only one, or the best one, I only want to make my own mark in the world, however big or small that might be.

Make the choice to consistently turn your envy into inspiration.

▣ EXERCISE

Write down as many things you can think of that have recently triggered you to feel envy. Once you have done that, for each one write an alternative inspired perspective that you can choose to attach to instead.

Envious thought:

....

....

Inspired thought:

....

....

SEEK OUT INSPIRATION

If you want to progress even further in your manifesting journey, then not only should you turn your envy into inspiration, you should **actively seek out inspiration. Seek out people who can inspire you and provide proof that it is more than possible to manifest anything that you desire.**

Remember that inspiration is high vibe.

For example, if you want to manifest launching a successful sustainable-clothing brand, look at other sustainable-clothing brands who have had incredible success to show you that it is possible.

> Looking for people to inspire you gives your conscious and subconscious mind proof that what you want to manifest is possible. This helps to remove any underlying doubts that it is not while helping you to enrich your visualization.

In Step 5: Embrace Gratitude (without caveats) (see page 109), I explained how integral gratitude is for our manifesting journeys. Envy and gratitude cannot coexist. When you feel jealous of someone else and of what they have, you cannot simultaneously be practising true gratitude for what you have. For example, you cannot be *wholeheartedly* grateful to have met your soulmate and be in a long-term committed relationship if you are feeling envious of your best friend's single-girl escapades and adventures. This is just another reason why gratitude is so powerful.

When we practise more gratitude and when we *really* sit in that space of complete appreciation for all that we already have, we can celebrate those around us without envy taking over. I can honestly say that since practising and embracing gratitude (without caveats) myself, I have never been more supportive of the people around me.

Here are the four steps you need to take to turn envy into inspiration.

1. **Become aware of it**
   To acknowledge our envy, we need to be mindful of our thoughts so that we can catch it when it comes.
2. **Remove the shame and judgement surrounding envy**
   Instead, practise self-love by offering yourself compassion, kindness and non-judgement.

3. Learn from it

If you find yourself going to judge another person, ask yourself, 'What is driving this judgement? What fear or doubt is driving this? What do they possess that I desire?'

4. Turn envy into inspiration

At every opportunity to feel envious of something or someone, you have an equal opportunity to reframe your perspective and turn it into an opportunity to feel inspired.

A final thought on envy: Remember when I said that self-love underpins every step of manifesting? Well, this couldn't be more relevant than here. The more compassion, non-judgement, love and kindness we can offer ourselves, the easier we will find it to transform our envy into inspiration. And the more we truly love who we are and the person we are becoming, the less likely it is that we will be triggered by the things that we see around us. When you love yourself unconditionally and when you are proud of the person you are today and the person you are becoming, there is no room for envy to live.

STEP 7

TRUST IN THE UNIVERSE

'The secret of getting what you want from life is to know what you want, and believe you can have it.'

NORMAN VINCENT PEALE

Once you know the life that you want to manifest, you've cultivated self-love, removed fear and doubt, overcome tests from
the universe, aligned your behaviour, embraced gratitude (without caveats) and turned your envy into inspiration, all that is left
for you to do is to have trust: trust that the universe will provide
you with everything that you need and trust in the magnificent
magic of manifesting.

This trust can be described as a 'knowing feeling'. It is knowing
that, even if you have no idea how it will happen, you just know
that it will. It is knowing, without doubt, that the things you
desire most *are* coming to you. It is this belief and unwavering
faith that will ultimately enable you to call in whatever it is you
want to manifest.

One of the biggest misconceptions about manifesting is that it
is about controlling your future. But manifesting is *not* about
control. Manifesting is about *surrender*. It is about knowing and
visualizing what you want, being proactive in reaching it but
then surrendering to the journey that will ultimately guide you
there. Remember when I said, at the start of this book, that
visualizing what you want is like putting your exact destination
into Google Maps? Well, imagine, then, that manifestation is
the computer program behind the app. You allow it to direct
you on which turns to take, which roads to avoid, which

highways to travel down and to help you get you back on track if you take a wrong turn. You don't attempt to control this process; you allow it to do its job while you do yours. So, to surrender to the magic of manifesting, you must trust in it in the same way.

Before I discovered manifesting, I viewed any kind of rejection as supporting evidence that I was unworthy or unlovable and I repeatedly allowed it to deter me from moving forward. I settled for less than I deserved because I doubted that the things I desired would ever come to me. I allowed envy to take over because I didn't believe that the life I wanted to have was one I could create for myself. I was forever standing in my own way, because I didn't have faith in a better future. Now, thanks to my unwavering trust in the universe and in manifesting, my life is very different: I see rejection as nothing more than a redirection to something better; I never settle for less, because I know that when I demonstrate high self-worth (by overcoming tests from the universe) I will be rewarded with abundance *and* I don't waste valuable energy on feelings of envy but instead seek to be constantly inspired. I know, from deep within me, that the universe has my back. I trust that it wants to provide me with the abundance it holds. I believe that the universe is generous and that it wants to provide for us *all*. It wants us to know our worth, to let go of what no longer serves us and to step into our power. I know that the universe wants the best for me, and I want you to know that it wants the best for you, too.

This final step is arguably the most powerful of them all. Not only does it help you to overcome challenges with greater ease, it empowers you to transcend fear and doubt, the two biggest blocks to manifesting. There is simply no room for fear and doubt to exist when you have full faith in the universe and its ability and willingness to provide for you.

FEELINGS OF TRUST, ASSUREDNESS AND UNWAVERING CONFIDENCE ARE ALL HIGH VIBE AND THEY ENABLE YOU TO EFFORTLESSLY ATTRACT ABUNDANCE INTO YOUR LIFE.

Trusting in the universe supports your manifesting journey in another way, too: it allows you to cultivate that magnetic attitude of gratitude that is needed for manifestation. How? Well, when we are *certain* that something is going to happen we can surrender to the journey of getting there. This, in itself, removes a level of worry, anxiety and stress, because it removes the constant question of '*How* will it happen?'. For example, let's imagine you are house-hunting: if you *lack* trust in it all working out the way you want it to, during your search you may find yourself constantly and desperately wondering, 'When will I find it?' and then feeling disappointed every time you see a house that isn't 'the one'. You might begin to panic that you won't sell your current property in time and you may find yourself having sleepless nights worrying about how it is all going to play out. The whole process could become an incredibly stress-inducing situation. However, if you have complete trust in the universe and trust that the perfect house will present it to yourself at the right time, you will be able to let go of all the low-vibe worry and doubt and instead give yourself an opportunity to indulge in feelings of joy and excitement about the search for your perfect home and the start of a new chapter. When you're not worried about *how* you are going to get somewhere because you just know that somehow you will, you can simply be more mindful in the present moment and practise greater awareness and appreciation for all that is already around you. This is how we really sink into that manifesting sweet spot that I mentioned in Step 5: Embrace Gratitude (without caveats) (see page 109): knowing what you want while being simultaneously and wholeheartedly grateful for all that you currently have.

Step 7 is integral to manifesting and it reinforces all the steps that come before it, but it is also the one that people struggle with the most. I will often hear people say, 'I'm doing everything I am supposed to and it hasn't happened yet. Clearly, this doesn't work for me.' They become frustrated and doubtful and begin to undo all the wonderful inner work they had committed to up until this point: they fall back into bad habits and begin to settle for things that compromise their self-worth because they no longer trust in the process. This usually happens because of one thing: *impatience*.

Impatience is the enemy of manifesting. This is because impatience interferes with a little something called *divine timing*. Divine timing is the timing of the universe, of an energetic force greater than ourselves. Trusting in divine timing is essentially a fancy way of saying 'I believe that everything happens for a reason.' When we trust in divine timing, we can surrender the need for control, for fixed timelines and for an urgency to rush our lives. Trusting in divine timing allows us to be present and mindful and to know that everything is unfolding in the way it is supposed to. It allows us to stay strong when things don't go exactly as we imagined. It allows us to find joy and beauty and contentment in the journey and not just in the destination. Divine timing is the essence of manifesting and we have to trust in it so that we can allow the magic to really do its best work.

For most people, divine timing is rarely given the space it needs to play out. What often happens is that they become impatient and begin to interfere with the process, and ultimately steer themselves off the path to their dreams in the hope of finding a quicker route. It's easy to understand why so many of us do this when we live in a world of instant gratification. It's as though we expect to manifest our dreams as quickly as we receive an online order.

The process of waiting for something is a huge test of our self-belief and self-worth. When something doesn't come to us straight away there is more room for our negative thoughts, limiting beliefs and insecurities to grow. Our instinct can be to lean into that negativity and to lower our vibration by allowing our fears and doubts to get louder. We may say things like 'I knew I wasn't worthy of it,' or 'I should never have believed I could have that for myself.' What happens then is that we try to heal the insecurity by finding something that can temporarily put a plaster over the self-doubt. For example, I had a friend who was single for a year. She had decided at this point that she was fed up with waiting to meet someone. She kept saying to me, 'Why isn't it happening?' I gently reminded her that, first, one year of being single really isn't that long, and second, it was clear that she was still full of fear and doubt. I told her that I believed she needed to focus on healing her past before she could call in her soulmate. But she did what many friends do when receiving advice; listened intently then chose to totally ignore it. She decided she couldn't be bothered to wait any longer, allowed her feelings of unworthiness to consume her and, unsurprisingly, went on to date someone who was never going to be able to offer her the emotional stability and commitment she deserved. She was interfering with her path to meeting her soulmate for temporary relief from being alone. It was only when she finally broke off that relationship and began to really commit to her own self-development and to raising her self-worth and let go of that need for it to happen at a particular time that she was able to meet the man who is now her fiancé.

The trick, really, is to **let go of waiting**. Waiting, especially when it verges on being 'desperate' for something to happen, lowers our vibration and disempowers us and our manifesting abilities. Make a choice not to wait but instead to live in the moment.

We come back, again, to the importance of letting go. Through-out this book, and throughout our manifesting journeys, we are asked repeatedly to **let go**: let go of the person we were, let go of the person we thought we should be, let go of our fears and doubts, let go of things that no longer serve our most empow-ered selves, let go of envy and, finally, let go of the need to control the exact direction of our paths. When we trust in our-selves and we trust in the universe, letting go becomes effortless.

> IN THE PROCESS OF LETTING GO,
> WE SURRENDER TO THE UNIVERSE.
> THEREIN LIES THE MAGIC.

I'd like now to tell you about how I used all the steps you have just learned to manifest this very book that you are reading now.

For as long as I can remember, I have loved writing. It has always been my favourite and most comfortable way to com-municate my thoughts, ideas and feelings. When I was at school, I would dream of becoming a published author and holding my very own book in my hands. I would tell people with complete certainty, 'I'm going to write a book one day.' But, as I entered a new phase of my life and began university, that dream was very much side-lined, as many of our childhood ambitions are.

A decade later, after I had discovered manifesting, realized my purpose and pursued my passion to become a self-development coach, the dream began to resurface. People would sometimes say to me, 'You should write a book,' and I would reply, 'Yes, I'd love to, one day.' The dream had re-emerged and I knew that I wanted to write a book – I was certain about that. But I wasn't sure when or how or what.

Then, last year, a book agent got in touch with me via Insta-gram. She asked me if I'd ever thought about writing a book and we started talking. In our conversations, for the first time, I was able to gain complete clarity on what the book was going to be: my 7-Step Guide to Manifesting. **Step 1 ✓**. Then, about two months after we started talking about putting together a proposal for her to take to various publishing houses, the agent had to step away from working together for personal reasons. 'This is probably a good thing as I didn't feel entirely ready anyway,' I thought. I stepped back and invested some time into looking at my own fears and doubt around writing a book – why did I not feel ready yet? I began to recognize some limiting beliefs that were stopping me from really believing I was capable, and then began to remove them one by one. **Step 2 ✓**. Then, around Christmas time, I made an internal decision: 'I am ready to write my first book.' I had simultaneously cultivated self-love and built my self-worth to such a place that I decided that I did not need an agent to help me find a publisher; instead, I was going to do it alone, with the magic of manifesting behind me. As I rang in the New Year, 2021, I wrote on my one-year vision board, 'Book written, edited and ready for publication.' I put it out to the universe. Then, I went on my Instagram and created a little Insta story that said, 'Hi, I am looking for a book publisher. Anyone who is interested in talking, please get in touch!' I aligned my behaviour by taking action, stepping out of my comfort zone and being proactive in moving forward with my visualization. **Step 3 ✓**.

A publishing house replied immediately; they were keen. I hadn't heard of the publishing house before, but they were well respected within the industry. I spoke on the phone to the lovely lady who had approached me on Instagram and, within a week, I had received my first offer. It was a really good offer. But when I spoke to them again, something in me just wasn't sure. I knew, in my heart, that there was one publishing house I wanted to sign with, and only one. It was the one that had published the book that first took me on my self-development journey, *Feel the Fear and Do It Anyway* by Susan Jeffers. The publisher I really dreamed of signing with was Penguin Books. Here was my test: an offer was on the table, but not from Penguin. I declined the offer on the Friday. **Step 4 ✓**.

The next day I met up with my good friend Olivia for a walk and told her about what had happened with the book deal. She said, 'Why don't you ask someone like Elizabeth Day for advice? She's published some amazing books – perhaps you could reach out to her on Instagram?' A lightbulb moment. I didn't know Elizabeth and I didn't feel comfortable reaching out to her out of the blue, but I did happen to know her agent, Grace, very well. I left Grace a voice note that night, and she replied explaining that the offer I had received was in fact a very good one for a first-time writer but saying she would have a think and let me know if she had any ideas on what I could do next. On Monday evening, as I was unwinding in the bath from a long day, my phone went. It was Grace. She said, 'Hey, Rox, so, I totally forgot, but I actually had a Zoom meeting scheduled in this morning with Ione, an editor from Penguin's non-fiction department. She said they're looking for some new material. Here is her e-mail address.' I smiled to myself. How serendipitous that she had a meeting in her diary with my dream publisher less than forty-eight hours after I had reached out. Still sitting in the bath, I typed out an email to Ione straight away. I had complete trust that the universe had presented me with this opportunity for a reason. **Step 7 ✓**. The subject line of the email was 'The Manifesting Book' and in it I wrote, 'Hi Ione, I got your email from Grace just now. To introduce myself quickly, I am a self-development coach and manifesting expert. Each month I host self-development workshops on Zoom, one of which is my 7-step guide to manifesting. I want to turn it into a book. Excuse the forward email but let me know if you want to chat. Happy Monday! Roxie x'.

Five minutes later, I received a reply.

Hi Roxie, Thanks for getting in touch. I'm so glad you did. Manifesting is something I've been talking about with my team recently and keeping an eye on. So, I am very interested and would love to find out more. How does Thursday at 9.30 a.m. work for you to discuss a little more? Thanks again for reaching out. Warm wishes, Ione.

About ten minutes into that meeting, I noticed something. There was a book on Ione's desk with a cover I recognized instantly: Susan Jeffers' *Feel the Fear and Do It Anyway*. I knew the moment I saw it that this was meant to be. Within a week we had made a formal agreement. I cried on the spot: Penguin would be publishing my first book – and I had found out exactly one year, to the day, from when I had hosted my first-ever manifesting workshop.

TRUST IS THE GLUE THAT HOLDS THE STEPS OF MANIFESTING TOGETHER.

As you begin to explore manifestation, look out for 'coincidences', or serendipitous moments, and for those times when you are thinking about something and it suddenly shows up for you. For example, if you're thinking about a song you want to hear and it suddenly plays on the radio, or if you think about someone you haven't spoken to for a while and they message you out of the blue. Take note of all these occurrences and allow them to help you strengthen your trust in the universe. Allow them to show you the powerful energetic force that exists in the universe and the powerful ability within you to create and alter your own reality. And then, when the things you want to manifest into your life begin to appear, see your trust strengthen tenfold and allow that to propel you even further into your manifesting journey.

EPILOGUE

When you began reading this book, you may have thought that manifesting was just about visualizing the things you want and then waiting for them to happen. I hope that, now, you are able to see and understand all the many layers of manifesting. I hope that after reading this book you see manifesting in the same way I do; not just as a magical force but as a self-development practice to live by. Manifesting does not just bring abundance into your life, it helps you to step into your power and unleash all the incredible potential within you.

At the core of manifesting is your self-worth, your subconscious beliefs about what you deserve and your capacity for self-love. Manifesting encourages you to be the best version of you that exists. It pushes you to step into your most authentic and empowered self and discover the inner strength that lives within you to overcome your limiting beliefs, your doubts, your fears and your insecurities. Manifesting asks you to let go of what no longer serves you and to remember that you can be anything you want to be.

Every single thing you do, day to day, is an opportunity for you to strengthen your manifesting power: the thoughts you choose to attach to, the way you nourish and fuel your body, the daily practices you commit to, the habits you create, the friendships you have, the behaviour you accept from others and the willingness you show to step out of your comfort zone. Everything you do is a demonstration of self-love, and every decision you make has the ability to raise your self-worth and drive you closer to your dreams.

In truth, the steps in this book are not to be approached one by one but worked through simultaneously. Each of the 7 steps in this book supports the others, and when you are able to master them all you will unlock the magic of manifesting.

You only have one life, and your job is to make it the best that it can be and to live a life that is filled with joy, love, purpose and fulfilment. It is time, now, to stop letting life just happen to you, and instead begin to recognize the infinite power within you to choose and create the exact life that you want to live and to manifest your best life.

SOMEONE ONCE TOLD YOU THAT YOU COULDN'T HAVE IT ALL.

I AM HERE TO TELL YOU THAT YOU CAN.

ACKNOWLEDGEMENTS

To Wade, none of this would have been possible without you. Thank you for absolutely everything.

To Leah, my soul sister, thank you for being the best friend I've ever had.

To all my family, I love you all more than words can say.

To Annie, for being by my side and helping me every step of the way.

To Amy Bailey, thank you for bringing my cover vision to life!

And finally, to every single person who has allowed me into their own self-development journey, who has come to a workshop, picked up this book or shared themselves within this amazing community.

SOURCES

p.10, Robin Sharma, *The Monk Who Sold His Ferrari: A Fable About Fulfilling Your Dreams and Reaching Your Destiny*, The Haunsla Corporation, 1997

p.24, Brian Tracy, *The Psychology of Selling: Increase Your Sales Faster and Easier Than You Ever Thought Possible*, Thomas Nelson, Inc, 2004

p.54, Don Miguel Ruiz, *The Four Agreements: A Practical Guide to Personal Freedom*, Amber-Allen Publishing, 1997

p.78, Mel Robbins, *The 5-Second Rule: Transform your Life, Work, and Confidence with Everyday Courage*, Savio Republic, 2017

p.81, John C. Maxwell, *Today Matters: 12 Daily Practices to Guarantee Tomorrow's Success,* Warner Faith, 2004

p.82, Oprah Winfrey, interview with Facebook COO Sheryl Sandberg, 2017

p.138, Norman Vincent Peale, *Positive Thinking Every Day: An Inspiration for Each Day of the Year*, Fireside, 1993

INDEX

W

Y

MANIFEST

NOTES

....
....
....
....
....
....
....
....
....
....
....
....
....
....
....
....
....
....
....
....
....
....
....
....

....
....
....
....
....
....
....
....
....
....
....
....
....
....
....
....
....
....
....
....
....
....
....
....
....
....
....
....
....
....

....
....
....
....
....
....
....
....
....
....
....
....
....
....
....
....
....
....
....
....
....
....
....
....
....
....
....
....
....
....
....

NOTES

....
....
....
....
....
....
....
....
....
....
....
....
....
....
....
....
....
....
....
....
....
....
....
....
....
....
....
....
....
....

....
....
....
....
....
....
....
....
....
....
....
....
....
....
....
....
....
....
....
....
....
....
....
....
....
....
....
....
....

....
....
....
....
....
....
....
....
....
....
....
....
....
....
....
....
....
....
....
....
....
....
....
....
....
....
....
....
....
....
....
....

....
....
....
....
....
....
....
....
....
....
....
....
....
....
....
....
....
....
....
....
....
....
....
....
....
....
....
....
....
....
....

....
....
....
....
....
....
....
....
....
....
....
....
....
....
....
....
....
....
....
....
....
....
....
....
....
....
....
....
....
....

....
....
....
....
....
....
....
....
....
....
....
....
....
....
....
....
....
....
....
....
....
....
....
....
....
....
....
....
....
....

....
....
....
....
....
....
....
....
....
....
....
....
....
....
....
....
....
....
....
....
....
....
....
....
....
....
....
....
....
....
....

....
....
....
....
....
....
....
....
....
....
....
....
....
....
....
....
....
....
....
....
....
....
....
....
....
....
....
....
....
....

....
....
....
....
....
....
....
....
....
....
....
....
....
....
....
....
....
....
....
....
....
....
....
....
....
....
....
....
....
....
....
....
....

....
....
....
....
....
....
....
....
....
....
....
....
....
....
....
....
....
....
....
....
....
....
....
....
....
....
....
....
....
....

....
....
....
....
....
....
....
....
....
....
....
....
....
....
....
....
....
....
....
....
....
....
....
....
....
....
....
....
....
....

....
....
....
....
....
....
....
....
....
....
....
....
....
....
....
....
....
....
....
....
....
....
....
....
....
....
....
....
....
....

....
....
....
....
....
....
....
....
....
....
....
....
....
....
....
....
....
....
....
....
....
....
....
....
....
....
....
....

....
....
....
....
....
....
....
....
....
....
....
....
....
....
....
....
....
....
....
....
....
....
....
....
....
....
....
....
....
....
....

....
....
....
....
....
....
....
....
....
....
....
....
....
....
....
....
....
....
....
....
....
....
....
....
....
....
....
....
....
....
....

....
....
....
....
....
....
....
....
....
....
....
....
....
....
....
....
....
....
....
....
....
....
....
....
....
....
....
....
....
....

....
....
....
....
....
....
....
....
....
....
....
....
....
....
....
....
....
....
....
....
....
....
....
....
....
....
....
....
....
....
....
....

NOTES

....
....
....
....
....
....
....
....
....
....
....
....
....
....
....
....
....
....
....
....
....
....
....
....
....
....
....
....